The **POWER** of
BOREDOM

WHY BOREDOM IS ESSENTIAL FOR
CREATING A MEANINGFUL LIFE

MARK A. HAWKINS

Cold
Noodle
Creative

Mark A. Hawkins

The Power of Boredom

Cold Noodle Creative

Softcover ISBN 978-1-7782546-3-5
Electronic ISBN 978-1-7782546-4-2

Cover & Text Design | Kristy Twellmann Hill
Art Direction | Fleck Creative Studio

DEDICATION

This book is dedicated to my parents. How a person comes to be who they are is a mystery, but no doubt my mom and dad were pivotal in my creation. While a short dedication is not nearly long enough to begin acknowledging this fact, I will attempt to craft a few poignant words.

To my mom, Susanne Hawkins, whose strength through a string of personal tragedies has not withered her vitality and compassion for others. I can only hope I would be so brave and intrepid as you.

And to my dad, Lee Hawkins, who left us way too early. I truly think that you were a writer at heart, but never got the chance. So I write this book in honour of your memory and hope it makes you proud.

I love you both.

The **POWER** of **BOREDOM**

PREFACE

"Mr. Hawkins, I'm bored." These were the few disheartening words spoken by one of my high school students that eventually led to the writing of this book.

It was a beautiful warm and sunny day in late spring and, as a break from the routine, I decided to reward my class for working hard by taking them outside to enjoy the weather. It had been one of the great pleasures of my childhood to just sit on the grass and stare at the sky, and I wanted our class to share the experience together.

My students jumped out of their seats in excitement the instant I announced that we would be going outside. Even the students who normally sat like zombies at the back of the class came alive with energy.

Walking past the other classes like a triumphant parade, we made our way outside to the field. I told them to relax and just stare at the clouds drifting by. I did the same thing myself.

Then it happened.

I sat up and looked behind me. Almost all the students were on their smartphones except for the one chatty girl who didn't have her phone with her that day.

I realized then and there that my students' diminishing tolerance for boredom was not only preventing them from learning effectively in class (as I'm sure my colleagues would attest to), but it was also preventing them from taking precious moments in their day to enjoy and learn about life. I also realized that I was part of the problem.

Teaching has changed in the past decade or so. Slowly, an unofficial requirement has developed for teachers: entertaining. If you struggle with finding a way to engage your class, it is indirectly suggested that there is something wrong with your teaching. But as teachers try harder and harder to keep classes exciting and fun, the worse the level of engagement gets. It is a never ending and deflating battle.

But my students were just the canary in the coalmine. Even I was not immune to my own growing intolerance for boredom. The ease of finding entertainment at our fingertips over the last two decades has almost imperceptibly been eroding our tolerance for sitting and doing nothing. We've all been sitting in a pot of hot water, slowly increasing the distractions and diversions in our lives, and we haven't realized that we're beginning to burn.

INTRODUCTION

Never before in human history has it been more important to embrace boredom and never have we been less tolerant of it. This is the irony and tragedy of our times. The funny thing about life today is that we are all actually profoundly bored, but because there are so many distractions, we don't even know it. It's a nagging feeling that we need to be constantly doing something with our time. It's always bubbling below the surface ready to boil over the second our time is free. Since the world provides so much distraction in the form of technology, social media, 24 hour news, and "keeping up with the Joneses," it's easy to just pop that lid back on the pot and hold it down as tight as we can. In fact, the busier we are, the more bored we are likely to be. But all this distraction and busyness does is create the illusion of a satisfying and meaningful life.

WHY LIFE IS FILLED BUT UNFULFILLING

You know what I'm talking about. Life is so busy and full of activity, yet we still feel lifeless, dissatisfied, and unfulfilled. The activities that fill our lives provide us with little satisfaction and fulfillment even though we try to convince ourselves otherwise. With a paycheque as our only solace, the daily monotony reduces us to walking zombies on a giant hamster wheel. It is no wonder that we live for the weekend when we can go out for drinks with friends, indulge in some takeout, or chill out at home and binge-watch Netflix. Think about that phrase for a moment: "living for the weekend." If you are living for the weekend, then all the grueling hours at school or work are endured just so that you can have a few hours of relief. Your life revolves around a couple of fleeting hours!

Over time, even the few hours of leisure that provide momentary fulfillment are drained of their pleasure and we are forced to look for something else to make us feel good.

We know that there is something missing and we go about trying desperately to figure out what it is. We frantically fill up our lives with more and more stuff hoping that the next thing we do will finally give us lasting satisfaction. We believe that there is some sort of final state or destination that will provide us with endless bliss. Maybe when we have enough money to buy the perfect home in the perfect location we will be satisfied. Maybe when we have a spouse and a family of our own we will feel fulfilled. Perhaps when we reach a certain level of spiritual enlightenment, we will no longer feel like there is something missing from our lives. Unfortunately, none of the things we fill our lives with are guaranteed to give us the life satisfaction we desire. So why is it that we feel so lifeless, dissatisfied, and unfulfilled when we are busier than ever before?

OUR LIVES LACK MEANING

We feel this way because the activities we fill our lives with are not providing the meaning that we crave, but we can't deny that we need meaning in our lives as much as we need food or air. We perform our jobs simply to continue the cycle of making money, paying for leisure activities to escape the stress of the job, and do this over and over again. The thing is, for many of us, neither our careers nor our leisure activities mean anything immensely compelling to us. Even though we may try to convince ourselves that our jobs are meaningful, our need to take extreme measures to "unwind" tells a different story.

We need a compelling reason for our lives. It is something that is just built into us. So we tirelessly search for the best way to live. We search for a profound, universal meaning that will guide us, and provide certainty and satisfaction. We flock to yoga studios, and meditation retreats that promise meaning and enlightenment. We convince ourselves that our work has a great purpose in the world, or that family is all we need. Yet, these methods fall short of providing the constant satisfaction and fulfillment we expected them to provide, so we busy ourselves again looking for something new to fill our time.

BUSYNESS KILLS LIFE SATISFACTION

In today's world, our attempts at living a meaningful life are stopped in their tracks because our time filling prevents us from discovering our own compelling personal meaning by truly examining our lives. We learn how to live a satisfying and fulfilling existence by closely examining our world and our own lives, yet we are so busy that we do not have the time to properly do this. Almost every spare minute we have is filled with either tasks to satisfy the increasingly demands of the world, or with leisure activities to escape the world. Our desperate need for meaning has led to a thriving industry based on "McEnlightenment" which, rather than helping us to explore our personal meanings and existence, scratch the surface of spirituality while promising inner peace and fulfillment after ten sessions. Of course, we flock to these places wondering if it is "the answer." Life is filled to the brim, but it's unfulfilling.

Our attempts to live satisfying lives are made even harder because we live at a time when there are endless distractions. As soon as we have a spare moment, we scroll through our social media feed, turn on the TV, or surf the internet. Such distractions play right into our desperate and endless search for meaning, but what we don't realize is that distraction is the death of meaning! This is because what we are really doing is avoiding boredom.

Avoiding boredom not only kills life satisfaction, it also leads to negative behaviours. We fill our down time with food, drink, drugs, and drama just so there is something (rather than nothing) going on.

Since we are constantly distracted with activities that provide pseudo-satisfaction, we never truly examine our lives. When we don't think about life, we passively live out the default version of life, whether or not it's right for us. We conform to a certain way of living that provides little to no personal meaning because we didn't consciously choose it. It's the default, dominant idea of a satisfying and meaningful life. We assume there is no other way to live because, if we're honest with ourselves, we haven't really thought about it. Even if we realize there are alternative ways to live, our modern world provides so many choices, options, and paths that it becomes dizzying and nearly impossible to choose. So how can we discover our own, personal compelling reason to live? We must allow ourselves to be bored.

YOU NEED TO GET REALLY, REALLY BORED

We are prevented from properly examining our lives because we are terrified of boredom. Boredom has become so intolerable in modern life that we will do almost anything to avoid it. Ironically, the boredom that we find so painful and that we will do anything to avoid is the very thing that we need to begin to live a satisfying, fulfilling, and zestful life. It is by embracing boredom and using it to learn about the truths in our lives that we can finally create a meaningful existence. Despite its horrible reputation, boredom carries the potential to help us create the most compelling life any human can expect to live.

Some of you might be thinking, "I wish I had time to be bored!" There is so much busyness and distraction that we have actually convinced ourselves of our lack of time. Sometimes we even glorify it. But we all have times in our day when there is nothing that we *must* do, or *want* to do. Much of our busyness and distraction has actually become a way for us to avoid times of boredom under the guise of getting ahead, or getting things done. We may convince ourselves that all of the activity and busyness in our lives is necessary because we need to keep up, or get ahead. When we are alone in the evening with nothing much to do we probably flip on the TV, surf the net, or mentally organize our schedule for the next day. These are the times that are crucial. Will you fill them up with trivial activities that add nothing to life, or will you use these times to begin to create an amazing life? These times of boredom are the perfect spaces to examine and change our lives.

When we learn to use boredom properly, it is a powerful vehicle for meditation and the ideal space to begin to create a satisfying life. During times of boredom, when we are not distracted by the world, we can begin to see and feel the truths of life, and the things that are holding us back from living a fulfilling life. Socrates said that an unexamined life is not worth living and, as you will see, boredom is the best time in our lives to begin that examination. Boredom is a special space in time that provides us with a bird's eye view of life. The examination that boredom allows helps us steer our lives toward the best road possible. Just as we would never begin a road trip with a muddy windshield, we should not live our lives before we have cleansed the space of boredom of what is preventing us from living meaningfully. Once we embrace boredom and learn how to harness its power, we can create our own compelling personal meaning—the key to a life of satisfaction and fulfillment.

PART I

UNDERSTANDING BOREDOM

"Profound boredom is in fact an essential authentic mood of great therapeutic value."
— Christian Gillian

Chapter 1

WHAT IS BOREDOM?

BOREDOM IS AN UNEMOTIONAL EMOTION

When you are watching any movie or TV show, you are sure to see a lot of anger, love, hate, fear, and sadness. These are the emotions that keep us glued to our screens to find out what happens next and whether you love them or hate them, these emotions keep our own lives engaging. Boredom is the exact opposite of these emotions. In fact, it is sometimes called the unemotional emotion because it lacks the fiery passion that the others do. It's not hard to see why boredom has been largely ignored as an important emotion until recently. In fact, think of the last time you were bored, didn't you instantly try to find something to do? But don't let it fool you. Boredom is the most important human emotion.

Emotions are reactions to what is going on inside and outside of us. External stimuli are things that happen around us that we process inside our minds. Depending on our past experiences, our minds react to a situation with certain emotions. Imagine running on a trail in the wilderness when you suddenly see a bear. Obviously, you'll feel fear. Internal stimuli such as thoughts about the past or future can evoke emotional responses just the same as something happening outside our bodies. Thinking about a big exam or an important interview will cause anxiety today. In both these examples, our bodies are reacting to some sort of stimuli. Boredom is the lack of any stimuli that is engaging. If there is nothing around us that is exciting or engaging, we feel bored.

THE SPECTRUM OF BOREDOM

When we are scrolling through social media at school or work, we are not very engaged with what is going on around us and so the pictures, articles, and other posts provide a temporary escape. The more engaged we are in something, the less bored we will be. So there is a spectrum of boredom with complete engagement or engrossment on one end, complete boredom on the other, and different degrees of both in between.

A philosopher named Martin Doehlemann refers to *situational* boredom. This is a mild form of boredom that we experience when we are doing an activity that we don't really feel like doing, such as sitting in a boring class or doing repetitive work. We also experience this type of boredom when we get tired of doing an activity, such as watching a particular TV show. I refer to this type of boredom as "full" because, we are doing things, but we aren't engaged. This type of boredom is eliminated by moving on to another activity that engages us.

"EMPTY" SITUATIONAL BOREDOM

We experience empty situational boredom when we are not engaged in any activities. In other words, when we're doing nothing. We experience this boredom when waiting for something to happen such as waiting to go to a party, waiting for a game to start on TV, or waiting at the dentist's office. Sometimes we experience more intense situational boredom. This can happen on weekends when there is nothing to do, or on lazy Sundays. In most cases, simply moving on to another activity, or checking out the latest social media feeds eliminates this boredom. Some of these situations may be more boring to us than others, but they all fall somewhere between total engagement and total boredom.

EXISTENTIAL BOREDOM

Total boredom has many names including profound boredom, extreme boredom, existential boredom, and life boredom. We experience "full" existential boredom when we are busy with our lives, but there is very little that interests us or engages us about it. We have all had busy days when all our regular activities provide us with no interest or stimulation. Even the leisure activities we used to enjoy seem dull and repetitive, and there is nothing that seems to hold our interest. I like to think of this type of boredom as just "going through the motions" of life. We often hear this type of boredom described as "being on a hamster wheel." Alberto Moravia, the Italian writer, describes existential boredom as the "disease" of the things that once gave life its vitality that have now "withered and died." This echoes Arthur Schopenhauer, the nineteenth century German philosopher, who said that existential boredom happens when we lose the capacity to find any object whatsoever for our desire, and there is no point to any action. Finally, full existential boredom can be defined as a withdrawal of meaning from everything in our lives. This is the type of boredom that is everywhere in our society today and it is what makes our lives dissatisfying, unfulfilled, and lifeless, even with the endless distractions and busyness. It is bubbling just under the surface of all our activity.

"EMPTY" EXISTENTIAL BOREDOM

We experience empty existential boredom when we are existentially bored as above but there is also nothing that we must do. It is when we have free time. This type of boredom is often the most painful because we are not doing activities that distract us from the meaninglessness of certain areas of our lives. This type of boredom is often linked to depression, anxiety, and destructive behaviours. Dr. Viktor Frankl, a psychiatrist who survived the Nazi concentration camps, said that this type of boredom is common in our society. He spoke about the "Sunday neurosis." It is an uncomfortable feeling that arises when we are not distracted by the busyness of our lives and it makes us feel that there is something missing. This often leads to "killing time" because the "empty" time is unbearably uncomfortable, and the free time that we have worked so hard all week for becomes too painful. At that point, we actually want the week to start again because it will distract us from the nagging feeling that something is missing. Have you ever been looking forward to some much deserved time off and then proceeded to fill it with watching hours of TV or spending most of it at the bar, or a combination of both?

Empty existential boredom is also felt by many of us in retirement. During this time, the meanings and personal identities that were provided by our jobs fade away, and we are left with a vacuum of meaning. The fact of the matter is that, retired or not, most of us are actually existentially bored, but we cover it up the second there is nothing to do. These times are uncomfortable, but are exactly when we need to stay with the boredom and not rush to fill it.

WHAT OTHERS SAY ABOUT BOREDOM

Anybody who has sat through a boring class or lecture knows that boredom is uncomfortable, but James Dankert, a neuroscientist, has found that contrary to what we might think, boredom actually causes us stress. While studying boredom at the University of Waterloo, he induced study participants to feel boredom and found that cortisol (a stress hormone) levels, were much higher when people were bored than compared to other emotions. This is partly why we do our best to avoid boredom like we do with other stressful situations. Psychologist Robert Plutchik has linked boredom to a form of disgust similar to what we might feel when we smell rotten food. It warns us to stay far, far away! Another psychologist, Stephen Vodanovich, found that when we are bored we are more likely to get angry. Other scientists in England even concluded that being bored could lead to an early death! They studied over 7000 people over 25 years and found that those who were bored were 40% more likely to have died by the end of the study.

You may be thinking, "Why would I want to be more bored if it's going to cause me more stress, more anger, and lead to an early death?!" The problem with all these studies and theories is that they focus on some of the negative consequences of the presence of boredom in our lives. They don't provide information about some of the positive outcomes that come from embracing boredom such as creativity, which I go into later in the book. They tell us nothing about why we react to boredom the way we do. Boredom causes stress precisely because we do not allow ourselves be bored. If boredom leads to early death, it is possible that drug and alcohol use and other destructive behaviours used to avoid boredom were significant factors.

All of our emotions have a purpose for us. There are no inherently "bad" or "wrong" emotions. It is when we dismiss or ignore our emotions, and what they are trying to tell us, that they become a negative force in our lives. All we know for sure from these studies is that they show us that boredom is immensely powerful. However, if boredom is going to be useful for us, we must dig deeper to understand what it is about boredom that makes it so powerful. A psychologist or scientist may approach the subject of boredom by seeking to define it and identify its characteristics. At the same time, a counsellor or philosopher may try to dig deeper to find out why we react to boredom the way we do and how we may understand its role in our lives. This is what we will do in this book.

BOREDOM AS SPACE

One way we can conceptualize boredom is by thinking of it as a type of space. When we think of space, we usually think of emptiness. But space is actually full of limitless potential. Take an empty room for example. This "empty" room is full of space, but it also has the potential to become almost anything. It could become a living room, a gym, or a storage room. It can literally become any room we can imagine. So before we fill space with something, rather than just being empty, the space contains limitless potential.

There are many who view space in this way. Of all the major spiritual traditions in the world today, Buddhist teachings are the most explicit about space. D.T. Suzuki stated that space has infinite possibilities and inexhaustible contents. That is, space can be nothing, anything, and everything, all at the same time. The Dalai Lama has spoken about *space particles* that reside in the spaces between things, and that make up the substance that causes everything in the universe. Similarly, this idea of particles that have the potential to be anything also shows up in recent quantum physics. Particles called *anomolons* have been found to take on the characteristics that their observers expect them to. Waves in space are found to turn to particles as soon as they are being observed. In other words, particles in space are not static by any means, but carry pure potential.

When we really think about this, the implications are pretty crazy! If these particles become what the scientists want or expect to see, they literally can become anything. This is what the space of boredom is like.

Boredom is the most powerful type of space because it is the space of pure potential for our thoughts and emotions. Boredom is the space that allows us to see through all the distractions of our modern, busy lives and into the true nature of our existence. Martin Heidegger, an early twentieth century philosopher, said that all the busyness and activity that has taken over our lives is actually "forgetfulness of being." This means that all the things that fill our lives are actually preventing us from truly examining our lives and our world so that we can make the best choices. In essence, we have forgotten how to live meaningful lives because we are so wrapped up in all the distraction of the modern world. Boredom is the space that allows us to take a break and begin to examine our lives. We can think of boredom as life's workspace. A place and time when we can examine our lives and tinker with it so that it is as satisfying as possible.

However, there are two problems that most of us face. First, because our lives are so filled up with activities, we rarely get the chance to be bored. Second, when we do experience boredom, we run away from it like it is the plague! So most of us find ourselves in a pickle: We are dissatisfied and the space of boredom is our opportunity to change our lives, yet boredom is so intolerable to us that we fill it up with whatever we can. Thus, before we can use boredom and access its pure potential to examine our lives, we have to cleanse it of all the stuff that is making us run away from it.

MEANING NEEDS SPACE

Another aspect of space that is worth exploring is the relationship between space and solid form. Most of us never consider that in order for things or objects to exist, there needs to be space. To clarify, imagine a single dot on a page. If we were to fill that same page with so many dots that there is no space between them, the dot no longer exists. It has no space to be a single dot. This example demonstrates that it is the relationship between the space and the object that helps us define both. They need each other to exist.

This is exactly why the space of boredom helps us to find meaning and life satisfaction. When our lives are always filled up with distractions and activities, there is not space for meaning to emerge. If we are always filling our time to avoid boredom, then we will never allow our lives the space to truly see the meaningful and purposeful aspects of living.

At the same time, boredom is filled with scary, uncomfortable things, which is why we try to run far, far away from it. The space of boredom can be so scary to us sometimes that we will go to great lengths to avoid it. We will even fill it with harmful, negative things that can potentially destroy our lives. Right now, you may already be feeling an underlying resistance to boredom. It may feel like a dark and scary basement to you. It is a dark, forgotten, unknown space and all you want to do is run back up the stairs to the comfort of the bright living room. But to live a truly fulfilling life, we must be open to what the emotion of boredom can teach us.

"Man finds nothing so intolerable as to be in a state of complete rest, without passions, without occupation, without diversion, without effort. Then he feels his nullity, loneliness, inadequacy, dependence, helplessness, emptiness."

— *Pascal*

Chapter 2
WHY WE AVOID BOREDOM

As I mentioned, when we begin to feel boredom, it can be like a dark and scary basement that we instinctually want to avoid. We don't know what it actually is that scares us, but we know that we have been avoiding it for years, and even the bravest among us is a little bit more cautious when we approach the door. When we open that door we will find creepy junk. But if we dig a little deeper, we will find the best treasures we can imagine.

BOREDOM IS A DARK BASEMENT

Most of us can never pinpoint why boredom is so painful because what makes it painful is mostly unconscious. Also, because we cover it up so quickly, we never have a chance to investigate.

When something is unconscious we don't know that we are thinking about it, or that it is affecting us. For example, we have all had times when we feel anxious, or sad but we can't quite figure out why. Somewhere deep down inside of us something is bothering us. Quite often the only thing that alerts us to an unconscious thought is a negative emotion that seems to come out of nowhere. At this point, we might try to find some way to cover up or avoid what we are feeling. On one night a few summers ago, I began to have feelings of anxiety and dread. There seemed to be no apparent reason for feeling this way. That same night, I had a dream that I was back at work teaching one of the most challenging classes I'd ever taught in my teaching career. Upon waking, I remembered the dream and realized that the feelings of dread and anxiety were caused by the uncertainties of the approaching school year. The dream made my unconscious thoughts and fears come to the surface.

We won't know exactly why we feel so uncomfortable with boredom until we examine it. Instead, all we can be sure of is that there is something within the space of boredom that is creating discomfort, anxiety, restlessness, and the need to do something. When there is nothing to distract us, those negative feelings are uncovered and are harder to avoid. However, these feelings signal to us that this is the perfect time to open the basement door and find out what is in that dark and scary space.

BOREDOM IS CULTURALLY TABOO

When we search the word "boredom" on the internet, it doesn't take long to discover that almost everything we find is negative. This can be a chicken and the egg scenario, but I believe we avoid boredom because we are taught it is something negative, not vice versa. For centuries, boredom has been characterized as something that breeds disgraceful behaviour and as something we should avoid. In western society, we have heard the common saying, "idle hands are the devil's workshop."

This societal prejudice toward "doing nothing" has continued into the twentieth and twenty-first centuries. We live in a cultural climate where boredom is associated with laziness, lack of direction, and even criminality. That is why from a young age, children are trained to "fill up" their time with as many activities as possible. A child doing nothing is scolded for not being productive in some way. We have been trained to think that we are doing something wrong when we are bored, and that we should always be engaged in either a productive or leisure activity.

In our society, being successful often means putting in the most time, doing the most work, or being the most likeable. Thus, we don't have time for boredom because we have to get ahead, and getting ahead often involves spending as much time as possible making ourselves better than the next person. If we accept this as truth, there is certainly something wrong when we are feeling bored. In fact, it has become fashionable to tell others how busy we are to emphasize our status and importance. Busyness has become a badge of honour!

This view of boredom is reinforced by the increasingly competitive nature of our economy. Companies and people are competing with each other to receive the most compensation possible from their product or service—so everyone tries to be the best. There is nothing inherently "wrong" with this system, but we must be aware of how it might impact our already escalated sense of guilt when feelings of boredom creep in.

WHY BOREDOM IS SCARY

Marie Josephine de Suin, a nineteenth century French writer, said that boredom is the fear of the self. This is because it exposes us to the societal norms and cultural expectations that we have not lived up to. The norms and expectations that we absorb into our lives are called worldviews, or philosophies of life. A worldview includes how we believe the world works, how best to live life, what to strive for, and what a "good" person is. However, many of the beliefs we have incorporated into our worldviews can actually lead to an unhappy and inauthentic life.

Boredom is a survival instinct that tells us to keep working towards improving ourselves. Consequently, when we are bored, our brains frantically search for ways in which we can do that. Not surprisingly, all the societal norms and expectations we learn automatically surface. This is because boredom wants us to keep improving ourselves, but the ways we know how are limited by our unexamined beliefs that are often problematic.

WHAT BOREDOM REVEALS TO US

We absorb worldviews throughout our lives, largely unconsciously, through family, media, school, work, and basically every interaction we have with the world. Since childhood, we have been ingrained with certain cultural and societal ideals that many of us strive to achieve. Through social media and other media sources, we are being bombarded by these ideals hundreds of times a day. Even though on some level we know that these are mostly lies and distorted truths, we still buy into the idea that we are all supposed to have hundreds of friends (because we all should be extroverts), have the latest gadgets, be wildly successful, and be having endless amounts of fun while doing it. So when our real lives do not match these ideals, we feel absolutely rotten. Ask yourself this question: In what aspects of your life are you not living up to your ideal? Are you making enough money to be considered successful? Are you married yet? Do you have enough friends?

What about your body? Do you look good enough? Do you have the right personality?

For me, the personality expectations have definitely impacted my view of myself because growing up, extroverts were almost always considered the ideal. In school, we are evaluated on how confidently we are able to present in front of a class. In recent years, I still run across articles such as "Ten Ways to Be More Outgoing", or "How to Overcome Your Shyness". The not-so-covert societal message is that introversion is less than ideal. That you are not quite right if you are not fully extroverted. Despite the fact that recent books, such as Susan Cain's *Quiet,* have made great strides in counteracting this idea, I still experience some feelings of shame whenever I see something like this because I know who I am is more introverted.

It is on quiet Saturday nights, or silent Sunday afternoons when there is space in our lives, that the societal expectations creep into the boredom and tell us we are not good enough in one way or another. These moments are painful and we may not even know why they are so unpleasant. Sometimes, when I am alone and bored, I have this vague, nagging feeling that should be out with friends, or trying to be more social, then I begin to feel negative about myself because of the deeply internalized beliefs that I'm not extroverted enough. The moment of boredom makes me feel that something is wrong. It isn't boredom that is wrong, it is the belief that arose in that space of boredom.

Some of us, when alone on a weekend night, begin to feel very depressed because we don't have a girlfriend or a date. We quickly spiral into thoughts that we will never find that special someone. Some of us find that anxiety surfaces in the spaces of boredom because we begin thinking that we aren't making enough money to be happy. Boredom can bring out that which is most painful and the ways we feel we are not meeting the ideals that we have accepted to be true.

LIMITING BELIEFS BOREDOM REVEALS TO US

Happiness is controlled by external events. The largely unconscious belief that external events control our happiness and life satisfaction is one of the more potentially toxic worldviews. When we hold this belief, we become slaves to the outside world and we are at the whim of other people and events that are out of our control. While external events certainly influence our life satisfaction, we must learn that satisfaction and fulfillment must start from within. We should resist the temptation to think we will be happier when others conform to what we want, or when our issues are resolved. Instead, we may work on developing *nonattachment* as it is described in Buddhism, and realize that all external things will fall short in providing us true contentment. In our moments of boredom, there is nothing outside ourselves to lift our mood. In this way, boredom shows us how much we have been relying on our environment to be happy.

The world is a competitive place. The view that competition is a natural way to live our lives can also become problematic. When we view life through a competitive lens, we find ourselves living in anxiety and fear. A competitive worldview implies that we must be better than others to be successful, valuable, and to have a satisfying life. Thus, when we feel we are not measuring up to others in one way or another, we may become depressed, anxious, or in a constant state of keeping up with the Joneses. This is a very stressful way to live. The problem is, the constant comparing that arises from a competitive worldview only breeds sameness and conformity. Most creative people realize this. It is the individual, unique creations of each artist that actually increases their competitive advantage.

While there are certainly competitive aspects to life, viewing it as the basis for how to live our lives can cause us pain when we are bored. This is because in moments of boredom, we should be competing! We should be doing something to get ahead of the next person. Instead, we can view the world as creative. When trees in a forest grow, in a way, they are competing with each other for water, soil, and sunlight. Yet, at the same time they are only concerned with their own creation, their own "tree-ness". The shift in thought from competing to creating changes how we experience boredom. Instead of feeling anxiety, we feel excitement because the boredom allows us time to explore creative ideas.

Every moment of life should be pleasurable. We often view boredom as the opposite of pleasure. This is why it is no surprise that when we are faced with boredom, the belief that life should be filled with constant bliss surfaces. We have been led to believe through many of the latest pseudo-spiritual fads and through the media that all of life should be pleasure, peace, and unending contentment. When our lives do not live up to this expectation, we become dissatisfied and disheartened. Boredom especially highlights this because when boredom enters our life, the inconsistency of this belief and what we experience causes cognitive dissonance. Inevitably, we become confused and disappointed. Instead, we must realize that there is no pleasure without pain, or love without hate. These contrasts must exist for us to experience them. Unfortunately, most of us immediately fill boredom with something pleasurable and never learn that boredom allows us to experience more fulfillment.

Personal Limiting Beliefs. There are also limiting beliefs that are more personal because they are more specific to what societal ideals affect us more strongly. Since they are highly personal, there are no examples that apply to everybody.

In my own life, I have struggled with my inherited idea of the ideal North American man. Even though many have told me that I look like the jock type, I was never really into sports or any of the culture that came with them. Instead, I was a daydreamer who loved Star Trek, was mildly introverted, and had sleepovers playing Dungeons and Dragons all night. While I was mostly happy with myself, there was certainly an underlying belief that my way of being was not the ideal way a man should be. I did not fit that mold so I was somehow lesser than.

Later in life, I tried to fit in with groups of guys who were into sports, cars, and other stereotypically "guy" things, but with no luck. I could never quite fit in. I just felt more like an outsider. During moments of boredom, I connected my beliefs with how I felt about myself. I began to realize that there was nothing actually lacking about me, but there was something wrong with the way I had been viewing the world. The boredom allowed me the space to sort out the long held beliefs that had been causing me pain and discomfort for so long.

THE DISCOMFORT IS NOT BOREDOM ITSELF, BUT WHAT IT REVEALS

Boredom exposes us to beliefs about ourselves that are toxic, limiting, and painful. Personal beliefs are things that we believe to be truths even though most of the time they are far from the truth. These deep seated beliefs about ourselves and the world have developed over time through our interactions with the world.

It can be very uncomfortable to confront these beliefs. For example, if we believe that we are not a smart person, boredom may force us to come face to face with this belief. During times of boredom, we may feel low about ourselves and even ruminate on all of the times we felt like a failure.

Thus, we don't feel negative because of boredom itself, but because of all the toxic feelings and beliefs come to the surface. In later chapters, I go over all the positive, meaningful, and fulfilling experiences boredom allows us to have, once we have cleansed it of all our negative beliefs and thoughts, and are ready to allow it in our lives. Most of the day we are busy going about our lives and our minds are on the tasks at hand such as work, school, groceries, calling the phone company, and the hundreds of other things that we do to live in this world today. In other words, we are distracted. But when there is nothing that we *have* to do, or nothing that we *can* do, there is a gap in our distracting activities, a space where these deep seated negative beliefs rush in. This is when we can explore all the limiting beliefs that are hidden in the space of boredom.

WHY BOREDOM IS REALLY, REALLY SCARY

Martin Heidegger, one of the most famous philosophers of the twentieth century, has said that boredom exposes a fundamental, scary truth about human existence: that everything in our lives and our lives themselves will eventually be drained of their meaning. The job that you are so excited about now will eventually lose all of its meaning for you. That goal that you have been striving for will soon seem empty. Boredom exposes the emptiness that all of us are longing to fill. Lars Svendsen says that boredom is the "inevitable falling short of the desire for the boundless fullness of life."

I'm sure you have felt this. You have a good life, a good job, a partner, and pretty much everything that you could want. But there are those times when you feel like there is *still* something missing. A void to fill. This is why so many of us today are flocking to the latest spiritual fads. We want to see if they will fill this void. We want to see if we have been missing the boat on fulfillment. We are looking for something that I like to call existential perfection. This is what most of the great religions promise when they talk about Heaven, Nirvana, or Valhalla. It is the desire to feel constantly full, engaged, meaningful, and peaceful. Clearly, humans have wanted this from the beginning of time.

We think if we can just find the right purpose in our life that total and complete bliss can be reached. We are looking for a guiding purpose that will always keep us engaged with life. When we are bored, at that very moment, we realize that there is no meaning in life compelling enough to fill that empty space in time. We realize that all there is, is boredom. No purpose. No meaning. Nothing. Ironically, boredom is the time when we feel farthest away from meaning yet, if we let it, it is the quickest and most powerful way to finding the most authentic and fulfilling meaning we can experience.

WE NEED FOOD, WATER, AIR, AND MEANING

Viktor Frankl, the eminent Viennese psychiatrist and survivor of the Nazi concentration camps, said that humans have two instinctual drives. The first is to survive, and the second is to find a purpose for survival. Another major reason why we detest boredom is because we are hardwired for the struggle for survival. It is the only thing that keeps us completely engaged. In the prehistoric past, there were times when we were on a constant search for food and shelter, and had to be vigilantly defending ourselves against all kinds of threats. We still have this basic drive to struggle for survival, but in modern society, most of us no longer struggle for survival in the same way. Lars Svendsen states that life is striving for existence and when existence is guaranteed, life lapses into boredom. In other words, when our basic survival needs have been met, we need to find another meaning for our lives. At this point, getting more money, food, or shelter will not add to our life satisfaction. Even though we might try to convince ourselves otherwise, buying a bigger house, taking more trips to Hawaii, or buying a more expensive car are all beyond our basic needs for survival. They will not give us the meaning we seek.

Dr. Frankl calls this need for meaning beyond survival the *will to meaning*. Carl Jung believed that the absence of personal meaning is one of the main causes of ill mental health. Similarly, Irvin Yalom, a renowned American psychiatrist, argues that the less meaning we have, the more psychological problems we may encounter. Thus, having a personal meaning to guide us in life is one of the most important aspects of our existence.

Dr. Paul Wong, a Canadian psychologist who has dedicated his career to the study of human meaning, says that what humans really want is to have is a satisfying and fulfilling life, and that this is provided by having a personal meaning that guides us in how we live our lives, what goals we pursue, and what type of life we think is worthwhile. Likewise, Joseph Campbell, the American mythologist who dedicated his life to studying the myths and stories of cultures all over the world, states that what we are really looking for in all we do is the experience of being alive. In other words, we are looking for meaningful engagement. So our personal meaning is a code to live our lives by, as well as what guides us to live the most satisfying, fulfilling, and zestful life.

LIFE IS ABSURD

Finding a compelling personal meaning is very important for our survival. But how can we dedicate our lives to finding a personal meaning and be sure it is the right one? We only need to look on social media to see the plethora of life advice, guidance, and top 10 ways to do whatever, to realize that there are literally millions of ways to live. It seems as if every different spiritual philosophy has a different idea about how to best live our lives. On top of that, mainstream society conflicts with what many of the world's great philosophies and spiritual traditions tell us. So what are we supposed to base our personal meaning on?

Albert Camus and Jean-Paul Sartre, both French philosophers and writers, described human existence as *absurd* because we seek meaning in life, yet there is no meaning or purpose that any human can be sure is actually real. There is no way we can know if one way of living or another will lead to satisfaction. There is no meaning that can completely fulfill our desire for existential perfection. To these philosophers and many others, this is one of the most fundamental problems of human kind, and one that is very difficult to accept. The fact that we need to have a personal meaning, and that we can never be sure that the meaning we choose is the best one, can drive us to madness!

DOESN'T GOD PROVIDE MEANING?

I'm sure some of you are thinking: what if I am a spiritual person who believes in a higher power? Doesn't that provide enough meaning to live a fulfilling life? Even the Medieval Christian monks struggled with their lives being sapped of meaning. These monks spoke of the *noonday demon* that struck about halfway through their day of devotion and drained them of any interest in what they were doing and made them feel like they wanted to move on to something else. Dare I say that their devotion to God was not enough to keep them engaged? That this meaning they ascribed to was not enough to keep their lives feeling full?

There may be some overarching meaning to it all. Some consciousness behind our existence. A God running all the shots perhaps. But the meaning of it is impossible to know. If those monks were absolutely sure that what they were doing was what they were supposed to be doing with their lives, then their doubts wouldn't exist, and the noonday demons wouldn't exist either. The following line from *Hitchhikers Guide to the Galaxy* has always helped me with this idea: "A human, from the planet Earth, was one of them, though as our story opens, he no more knows his destiny than a tea-leaf knows the history of the East India Company." In other words, we may all be part of God's plan, or part of another universal force, but there is absolutely no way we can know for sure what that plan is or what our role is in it.

When we accept absurdity, two other troublesome existential truths become apparent. The first is the realization that we are free and responsible to choose how we live with absolutely no guidance or guarantee. The second is that we all have a finite amount of time in which to find the best way to live our lives. The fact that we will all die sooner or later increases the urgency and the anxiety around finding personal meaning.

Now that you understand why boredom is so terrifying, you're probably asking yourself, "Why the heck did I read this chapter? Why can't I just keep living the way I have been with all my distractions?" Our reactions to these scary truths in boredom can destroy our lives more than the truths can. In fact, most of our misery and dissatisfaction stems from our fear of boredom.

"Boredom is the root of all evil."
— Soren Kierkegaard

Chapter 3

DESTRUCTIVE REACTIONS TO BOREDOM

Bertrand Russell, the Cambridge trained philosopher of the twentieth century, has claimed that much of the evil in the world has been caused by our flights from boredom, but that boredom is not evil in itself. From wars of world domination to the most inconsequential tiff with our neighbours, our strong need for constant engagement to cover the pain of boredom has driven much of our negative and destructive behaviours. So while you can't unlearn what we read in the last chapter, you can become aware of the common destructive reactions that we use to fill the space of boredom.

FILLING TIME AND KILLING TIME

Filling time and killing time is the most common way we cover up the discomfort of boredom. We fill the space of our boredom with the easiest and most pleasurable activity that we have access to. Within this category are such activities as watching TV, shopping, surfing the net, playing video games, having a couple drinks, reading, or cleaning the storage room (when it doesn't need to be cleaned). These are any activities that we don't need for survival in the modern sense of the word such as going to work, school, making food, having shelter, or pursuing a goal. Most of the time these activities have little importance in our lives other than as a means of filling the time between more meaningful or important areas of our lives.

Filling or killing the spaces in our lives with these activities is an indication that the boredom is only mildly uncomfortable. It may be a reaction to our societal prejudice against boredom, or the boredom may be a small space between otherwise meaningful parts of our lives. Thus, the more meaningful and satisfying our lives are, the less painful our boredom will be.

Filling time and killing time is the least harmful form of diversion. All of us fill time or kill time in some way every day. There are times when these types of activities are necessity for giving our minds a break from the stress of more complex parts of our lives.

However, these types of diversions become destructive when they distract us from examining our lives and, consequently, prevent us from creating a satisfying and fulfilling existence.

BOREDOM CAN CAUSE ADDICTION

When the easy, pleasurable activities begin to consume more and more of our time, they become increasingly destructive and may even lead to addiction. Bruce Alexander, a Canadian psychologist, defines addiction as an "overwhelming involvement with any pursuit whatsoever that is harmful to the addicted person, to society, or both." This highlights the consumptive characteristic of most addictions, meaning that we are taking in pleasure through one of our senses.

When an activity that we have used to fill our boredom becomes an addiction, it usually indicates that the space of boredom has become more painful and so we need more powerful distractions to cover it up. As a teacher, I have observed, first hand, the teenagers whose harmless video game playing slowly advanced to becoming full-blown addictions that threatens other important areas of their lives. Early on, they could take or leave the games and spent only an hour or two playing them. However, as the reality of poor grades and pressures from all sides began to rise, they would be sleeping during class because of their all night video game addiction. Needless to say, this had a destructive effect on their academic and social life. So while there is certainly a behavioural aspect to addiction, it usually begins as a way of covering up increasingly painful emotions that are strongest in the spaces of boredom.

SOCIALLY ACCEPTABLE ADDICTIONS

Sometimes we do not recognize addiction in our lives because it is socially acceptable. Most recently, I have noticed the increasing numbers of people who are addicted to extreme forms of physical activity such as ultra-marathon running. While I certainly advocate for being responsible for one's health, it seems unlikely to me that such extreme physical exertion is healthy. Of course, upon researching the origin of the marathon, we quickly find out that the first marathon runner in Ancient Greece drops dead at the end! The problem is that many of these addictions are tolerated and even encouraged by society. Other examples include shopping, workaholism, and addiction to exercise. These reactions to boredom can be the most dangerous because we are often encouraged to fill our time with them. When they take over our lives, we may even be rewarded by society.

WE MAKE OURSELVES EXCESSIVELY BUSY

One of the most acceptable ways of covering up the pain of boredom is through compulsive activity, or excessive busyness. In fact, in recent years, our busyness has become dangerously intertwined with personal and societal value. Irvin Yalom refers to this as "a pattern of frenetic activity that so consumes the individual's energy that the issue of meaning is drained of its toxin." When there is no time in our busy schedules to experience boredom, then we will never have to experience the pain of unmet societal expectations, negative beliefs about ourselves, and absurdity.

While any activity can become compulsive or excessive, we usually become excessively involved in activities closely aligned with dominant cultural norms such as getting ahead at work, or accumulating wealth. Some of us fill up all our spare time doing extra work at our jobs and literally spend twelve to fourteen hours a day at the office. This is usually justified under the guise of a getting ahead, safety and security, or keeping up with the Joneses. Some of us may convince ourselves that we love our jobs, or that life is just like that these days. But more often than not, busyness is another sophisticated way of distracting ourselves from the pain of boredom.

Excessive busyness can take other forms as well. For example, we may compulsively fill our time with people. While we all need to have meaningful social interactions, socializing may also become another activity we cling to as a way of avoiding the space of boredom.

Excessive busyness does not have to be focused in one particular area either; it may look like a combination of all sorts of activities. However, the common thread remains that we have little to no time that is "empty." If we are excessively busy in our lives, boredom becomes extremely unpleasant. In our culture, having nothing to do means that there is something wrong with us. Eventually, the effectiveness of our compulsive activity in its ability to push boredom away dwindles. For example, a workaholic who loses their job is suddenly faced with hours of empty space that becomes very difficult to cope with. Excessive busyness is an easy form of escape to fall into because there is always something we could be doing.

WE TRAVEL TO AVOID BOREDOM

We all love a good vacation and the change of environment and pace are, to some extent, necessary in our hectic world. But when we begin to itch for another vacation the minute we get home from one, then we may have become a compulsive traveler. Compulsive travel sometimes known as "wanderlust" is effective at alleviating boredom because we are always experiencing something new and exciting. New cities, new people and new adventures keep us very engaged. When we begin to tire of a place, we can just move on to another.

Many of us cannot tolerate being at home when we are not at work or at school. The minute there is a stretch of down time, we are on a plane and don't return until the day before the work begins again.

I was not immune to this. After teaching in Korea for about two years, my wife and I returned home to Vancouver and, almost immediately, we both wanted to return to Seoul where everything was new and exciting. Home just seemed so boring. So we need to ask ourselves if we really love to travel or if we are avoiding the boredom and all it reveals to us at home.

WE ENGAGE IN RISKY BEHAVIOUR

Extreme sports have become more and more popular in recent years because they bring us to the brink of death. Coming close to death is never boring. Bungee jumping, cliff diving, base jumping, and sky diving all have inherent risk of immediate death, but there are even those whose weekend entertainment is getting involved in as many fights as they can. I remember a group of teens in high school whose main source of excitement was shoplifting from the local convenience stores. They would even plan hours in advance, choosing which jackets and pants would be best to covertly stuff things into, which routes to take, and how to distract the cashier. Gradually, they became more and more risky. Risky behaviours can be anything that involves some sort of risk of harm and we usually need to increase the risk over time.

WE CREATE DRAMA

It is not always the excitement of travelling or fighting that we use to escape boredom. Many of us create drama in our lives just to keep ourselves engaged in life. Life always seems more exciting when you have some sort of enemy or something to fight against. Creating drama in our lives mimics the survival instinct that was required in the past when we had to fight for our lives.

A classic example of this is when neighbours practically go to war over a couple of inches of fencing and an overgrown hedge. Another common example occurs every day in high school when a group of people dedicate their energy and efforts to bringing down one person outside the group. Even the everyday gossip and drama on reality shows provide a temporary escape. However, these seemingly minor ways of distracting ourselves can give way to more extreme and dangerous actions as the need for drama increases.

WE GO ON CRUSADES

An extreme form of creating drama that may indicate that we unconsciously feel our lives are meaningless is *crusadism*. Irvin Yalom defines crusadism as the need to seek out and dedicate ourselves to what we think is an important cause, usually fighting against something. There always seems to be a war on something today. On the surface this may seem perfectly fine, perhaps even noble, but there is a difference in becoming involved in a cause because we truly believe in it, and devotion to it as a reaction to the painful space of boredom. When we become dedicated to a particular cause, we often go back to our regular lives after the issue has come to a resolution. On the other hand, the crusader may choose to continue on with a failed cause, or find another cause to occupy their time.

According to Erich Fromm, a social psychologist, extreme forms of *crusadism* have been linked to destructive political and social movements like Nazism and the more recent jihadist movements against the west. Even in the west, I find it interesting that the United States has always had some sort of enemy. First, it was Hitler and the Japanese, and then it was the Soviet Union and communism. After the USSR collapsed, the new enemy was in the Middle East. Perpetual war means perpetual engagement and distraction from the space of boredom.

IS BOREDOM AWARENESS A MORAL OBLIGATION?
While not all destructive behaviours are a result of a flight from boredom, if we are not aware of our reactions to boredom, we run the risk of increasingly destructive behaviours that can jeopardize

our lives and world. This is especially the case now, in a world that has less and less tolerance for boredom.

Embracing boredom and learning about it is a moral imperative because our tolerance for boredom is diminishing. What atrocities are we willing to commit to flee from it? If boredom is the ground from which much of good and evil spring, then we have an obligation to be aware of it and our reactions to it. Boredom is a fundamental driver of human behavior, and everyone should learn how it affects their lives.

PART II

THE POWER OF BOREDOM

"When boredom strikes, throw yourself into it,
let it squeeze you, submerge you, right to the bottom."
— Joseph Brodsky

Chapter 4

BOREDOM IS A POWERFUL FORM OF MEDITATION

Thus far, we have discussed why and how we try to escape from boredom. This awareness is key to beginning your journey towards a fulfilling life. Moving forward, if we want to transform our lives and live with the most meaning and purpose possible, we must stay with our boredom to open ourselves up to what it may reveal to us. Boredom is the perfect space and time to begin examining our lives and existence. In fact, it is so conducive to life examination that it is similar to meditation.

WHY BOREDOM AND MEDITATION ARE SIMILAR

Traditional Buddhist meditation is a practice designed to experience the nature of existence. Practicing meditation is supposed to help you develop insight into suffering, impermanence, and the concept of no-self. During meditation, a person attempts to unlearn everything they know about things, people, and existence and try to see them as they truly are. Some forms of meditation also help us to experience the connectedness of all things. At the deepest levels, the goal of meditation is to experience the emptiness and nothingness from which all things are created. A person who is able to see the truth of existence will then be able to live a more enlightened, and presumably, better life.

Boredom is an ideal vehicle for all these things and more. Martin Heidegger, the German philosopher who studied the nature of existence, claimed that boredom is a profound mood through which the nature of existence presents itself. In fact, he called it the most essential form of *attunement* to being and existence. When we are attuned to something, or tuned in, we can hear what it is saying. When we tune in to a certain radio station, we hear what it has to say and which songs are being played. Heidegger states that boredom allows us to be tuned into the nature of existence and, therefore, helps us to hear what it has to say.

He also called the state of boredom *mindfulness of being* because it is the only time when we are not distracted or *forgetful of being*. He refers to this as *being-here* versus *being-away*. When we are distracted with everyday activities, we are actually away from real life. In fact, Heidegger went as far as to say that if we take the dominant cultural ideals of life seriously by getting a well-paying job and working our way up in society, we are actually living an inauthentic life of diversion. Thus, boredom, which is the absence of diversion, is the best method for pursuing an authentic existence that provides life satisfaction.

BOREDOM IS A WINDOW INTO EXISTENCE

Boredom shows us the emptiness, pointlessness, and nothingness of all phenomena without dogmatism. It strips everything of its meaning to us. Imagine for a second that you are the last person on earth and you are stranded on a desert island. There is no society left, no jobs, no other people, not even any animals. There is nothing at all to define you or guide your actions. You are all there is. After reflecting on this for a while, you may reach the conclusion that there is really no point to any action at all. Even surviving! There is no point in building a boat to get to another place. There is no point in searching the world for other people. Sure, you could occupy yourself for a while, but you will eventually realize that the only point of existence is existence itself. And this existence is meaningless. It now becomes obvious that everything that you do on that island is just a distraction from the reality of your existence.

At the end of the movie *Gravity* starring George Clooney and Sandra Bullock, Clooney's character, astronaut Matt Kowalski, is doomed to float out into space forever. This is a powerful image in the movie. Most of us would find this terrifying. The astronaut no longer has any purpose or meaning for anything he does. Everything becomes meaningless. What would be the point of reading a book? What would be the point of worrying about your weight? The only point of doing anything would be to distract yourself from the nothingness of your existence that is now floating off into space.

Similarly, Anny, a character in Jean-Paul Sartre's famous book *Nausea* is obsessed with perfect moments of the past. This obsession arose because she was avoiding the space of boredom. She echoes the feeling of nothingness when she proclaims "I shall never again meet anything or anyone that will inspire me with passion." She believes that her life is over.

Lucky for us, it isn't likely that we will float out into the nothingness of space. However, this is exactly what boredom feels like. Every action, object, and thought lacks any purpose or meaning in itself. A lifelong experience of nothingness isn't the goal for practicing mindfulness or allowing boredom. Instead, both boredom and mindfulness are glimpses, or short forays, into existence from which you can gain insight and then return to the world. However, allowing boredom in our lives can be more powerful for learning about the nature of existence and helping us to achieve life satisfaction.

BOREDOM: BEYOND MINDFULNESS

During my research for this book, I read some academic articles that actually presented mindfulness as a cure for boredom. I realized this concept hit on something important. Mindfulness is sort of a gentle engagement. In other words, it is a cure for boredom because it subtly reintroduces engagement into the space of boredom. It is another way of distracting yourself from boredom! This brings to light that the practice of mindfulness, while considered a form of meditation, is still slightly engaging and it doesn't necessarily create a space that is completely purged of meaning. Mindfulness is practiced for its benefits related to emotional and mental health issues from stress and anxiety to identifying and changing negative thought patterns. In addition, it is used as a means to increase awareness of our avoidance of the now, and bring our minds back to the present moment. On the other hand, boredom is a complete lack of engagement. A complete lack of meaning. So while mindfulness gets us pretty close to nothingness, boredom gets us even closer.

Another way to look at this is that you can get bored of doing mindfulness, but you cannot get bored of boredom. Boredom is the lowest common denominator of mood, feeling, or experience. In fact, getting bored of boredom is a paradox. But while most proponents of mindfulness would avoid getting bored, the shift from mindfulness to boredom may actually be the best time to gain deeper insight into self and existence.

Mindfulness is an attempt to take away the meaning we give to things, but boredom is the meaninglessness of things. In a way, boredom is a natural kind of meditation that lifts the thin veneer of reality off all things. This is because when we are bored, we keep trying to fill it with meanings. When we allow boredom to happen, we allow the meaninglessness to surface.

Mindfulness is also intentional, and when we do something with intention, it automatically has a purpose. The practice of meditation helps us to experience nothingness and enlightenment, but when we have an intention, our own definitions and ideas fill the space. When we intentionally seek enlightenment or peace in mindfulness, we convince ourselves that we have found it. In mindfulness, we tell existence what it is. We define it. We place meaning on it. But boredom is not intentional. We are not defining its parameters. We cannot tell it what to say. It washes over us. It is the nakedness of existence that invades our mind and soul. That's why it is uncomfortable.

Most of the time, the practice of mindfulness is *for something* whereas boredom simply *is*. Mindfulness is the *purposeful* search for nothingness, but boredom is nothingness that surfaces within you. Ironically, if you search for nothingness, you will never find it. Nothingness finds you. You cannot find it. Allowing moments of boredom is imperative to experiencing nothingness.

BOREDOM VERSUS STILLNESS, SILENCE, AND QUIET

The ideas of inner stillness, silence, and quiet have become popular terms used for describing the idealized states we are trying to achieve when practicing mindfulness. However, there is a danger in leaving it there.

As I mentioned before, there is some meaning present when we practice the form of meditation we call mindfulness. This is because it is intentional. When we practice mindfulness and seek answers from the universe about how to allow more peace into our hearts or how to deal with our negative emotions, our answers may come from the same meanings and preconceptions we had when we began the mindfulness practice. However, we can't intentionally create boredom. Boredom is when you are practicing mindfulness, get an answer (or not), and start feeling restless and antsy, itching to go attend to something else. Boredom is the deep discomfort you feel because nothingness has emerged. If we believe that the answers that mere stillness and silence give us are true, we will happily stop our mindfulness practice before we receive the valuable lessons from the void of boredom. The moment you get bored of stillness and silence is when it becomes most valuable.

YOU CREATE TRUE MEANING

Joseph Brodsky, the Nobel Prize winning author, says that we must submerge ourselves into boredom, right to the very bottom, because it will teach us the most valuable lessons of life. However, the purpose is not to stay in the deep space of boredom, but to grasp the expansive possibilities of being, and then leave. Christian Gillian, a philosopher from the University of London, says that boredom gives us the tools to live satisfying lives. But we can't fully grasp the lessons contained in it just by reading about them in this book. They have to be felt all the way to our core. Just like you can't fully express what love is in words, you can't fully express the profound lessons of boredom. But I will give it a try.

Boredom reveals the limitations of existence and tells us that we should abandon our search for a perfect existence. In fact, the search for a perfect existence is what distracts us from really living well. When we endlessly search for the "perfect" answer to life, we are actually stopping all the possibilities of our lives from being revealed to us. Ironically, realizing that there are limitations to our existence, that there is no universal meaning, and that there is no perfect form of existence, actually opens us up to almost limitless possibilities.

Once boredom washes over you, you begin to realize that you are completely free, except from freedom itself! This means that *you* are the one who must give everything in your life a meaning, because meaning will not exist otherwise. It is boredom that makes us realize that the world and all of existence demands that you attach meaning to it. Boredom provides the clarity to see that the meanings we buy into are completely arbitrary and assigned by someone else. Pulitzer Prize winner Ernest Becker says that our culture provides a structure and dogma for us to find meaning, just like any religion would. He says, "society is and always has been a symbolic action system, a structure of statuses and roles, customs and rules for behaviour designed to serve as a vehicle for earthly heroism," or meaning. Boredom exposes to us the arbitrary nature of this system.

BOREDOM EMPTIES US, THEN FILLS US UP AGAIN

Boredom dissolves your identity and selfhood so that you can build it up again yourself. Heidegger says that boredom is the perfect space for letting go of your identity. If you are deep enough into boredom, you realize that your identity is actually made up of arbitrary meanings assigned by you or your culture. You may see yourself as a mother, father, lawyer, teacher, or spiritual leader, but if you were stranded on a desert island and are the last person on earth, these identities fall away because all the relations and comparisons that created those identities fall away. Boredom makes you realize that identity is fluid, and that you are not locked into a particular way of being.

Anny, the character from Jean Paul Sartre's book who I referred to earlier, was convinced that she would never again feel that anything was meaningful. She was totally bored. We can imagine that she felt her life was pretty much over. This is why Nietzsche referred to boredom as *death within life.* Interestingly, when we reach this level of boredom and let it submerge us, we begin to realize that the only reason we feel uncomfortable within the depths of boredom is because our view of existence was very limited going in. Whenever Anny was bored, she distracted herself with memories from the past. Perhaps if Anny had allowed herself to go deeper into her boredom, she could have seen the expansive possibilities of her own being.

HOW TO ALLOW BOREDOM INTO YOUR LIFE

In the past, there were a lot more spaces of time when boredom could enter. After the day's activities, there were more moments when people could experience boredom alone or together. Today, there are a plethora of easily accessible distractions that make it easy for us to distract ourselves for every minute of the day before we sleep. Thus, we must make a conscious effort to allow moments of boredom to enter our lives.

Just like it is with any emotion, we can't purposefully create the emotion of boredom within us. However, we can allow the conditions that make it more likely to happen. We can reduce the amount of distractions and diversions in our lives. Instead of watching two hours of Netflix before going to bed, turn off the TV, put your smart devices away, and just sit in silence for a while. This is the perfect time to allow boredom in because all our daily tasks for the day are done and there is nothing to do until the morning. When we do this, we create our own desert island or become an astronaut floating in space. All our purposeful activities from the day are gone and nothing demands our engagement again until the morning. Within even the shortest moments of boredom, the seeds of profound meaninglessness and nothingness begin to emerge.

"It is through boredom that we are truly equipped to reach satisfaction, openness to the world, and a sense of thauma (awe)."
— *Christian Gillian*

Chapter 5
TUNING IN TO BOREDOM

Boredom is a powerful space in time that allows the nature of existence to emerge. It is the presence of nothingness and emptiness that surfaces at times. When boredom arrives, we should not let it slip away, or distract ourselves from it. Instead, we can learn how to harness its power.

THE DIFFERENCE BETWEEN DISTRACTION AND NECESSITY

Throughout the day, it can be hard to tell the difference between something you actually need to do, and something that is just a distraction from boredom. If you have just eaten dinner, yet feel the urge to eat something else because you are home alone on a

Saturday night, you are eating to fill the boredom. If you spend two hours on the internet "looking something up" during your spare time, you are likely distracting yourself.

The problem is that there is always something we could be doing. That's why today's world is often called the age of distraction. If you have two spare hours you might as well get some cleaning done right? Or get a head start on that project at work? Isn't that the efficient, productive thing to do?

The first step towards differentiating distraction from necessity is recognizing when you are prone to boredom. For most of us, these times are in the evenings or on the weekends. I am most prone to distracting myself from boredom in the couple of hours before I go to bed. This awareness alone is half the battle in creating your spaces of boredom.

A second step could be to write down the ways that you usually fill the spaces of boredom during these times. If you find yourself doing one of these activities, the awareness can help you to stop and ask yourself, "Is this necessary, or am I just avoiding boredom?"

In addition, we must resist the urge to get ahead on any task. Ironically, we convince ourselves that we are being productive and efficient to save ourselves time down the road, yet as soon as there is extra time again, we fill it with other tasks. This extra time never seems to come. This brings to light the fact that "getting ahead" is essentially an excuse we use when we are really avoiding the spaces of boredom.

It can be really difficult to tell if something is a necessity. This is because it is personal. I like to ask myself what the consequences are of not doing something. Sometimes, this can help us to discern the importance of the task at hand. Also, if you find yourself feeling that everything is necessary, then that may be a warning sign. This feeling is usually accompanied by a feeling of being rushed or anxious when there actually isn't any immediate reason to rush.

We must also be aware of restlessness and the incessant search for something to do. There were times when I have wandered around the house in a futile attempt to find something that will spark my attention. It was very subconscious. Only after opening the kitchen cupboard ten times and scrolling through social media for ten minutes, I realized I was intensely bored, and was trying to avoid it at all costs.

ARE YOU RELAXING OR JUST DISTRACTING YOURSELF?

There are times when, yes, we do need to scroll through social media for a while with a glass of wine to wind down after work. There is no doubt that some of the diversions we have are absolutely necessary. However, we need to be aware that we can become dependent on them when we are using them to avoid boredom. It usually takes about half an hour or so to come down from negative feelings such as stress, or anxiety, so when we find that we are consistently grabbing our smart device when there is a space in time between activities, we should ask ourselves what the purpose is.

STRATEGIES FOR ALLOWING BOREDOM

Once we are aware of when an activity is a necessity or a distraction, we can consciously create spaces of boredom in our lives. One of the most effective ways to do this is to leave that last couple of hours before bed to do nothing. However, we can create spaces of boredom at any time that works for us.

Scheduling times to stay with your boredom is important, especially if you are a busy person. If you schedule the space, you are less likely to try to fill it with diversion. Again, I like to schedule the last couple hours of the evening a couple of days a week, but you can use the first hour of the day if you prefer.

It doesn't matter how busy you are, you can still find time to allow some boredom. If you're are waiting at the dentist or waiting in a line, instead of pulling out your phone, you can allow those few minutes to let boredom wash over you. Maybe find the most unengaging room in your home to sit in.

It is also important to catch boredom when it comes. Sometimes even when you create spaces of boredom, it may not happen. It is an emotion after all. An important clue that there is an opportunity for boredom is when you feel the discomfort of restlessness. As soon as you feel a twinge of restlessness, you should immediately stop and do nothing. This will be uncomfortable, and may even be scary, but it will be fruitful.

BOREDOM IS FLUID AND ELUSIVE

Boredom does not always come when we make the space for it. When it does come, it can fade in and out. We have to be patient with it. We can't expect it to reveal the secrets of the universe to us right way, although it might. A possible scenario could be that you begin feeling intense restlessness, then loneliness, and the next moment you are hit with a profound insight about your life. Boredom exposes the nature of existence, but only when we stay with it for a while.

Unlike some forms of mindfulness, we are not trying to place our focus on our bodies, minds, or breathing. Instead we should just be aware of and freely allow all the emerging thoughts and feelings to happen. Let them all wash over you. Remember that all kinds of thoughts, fears, and feelings will come into the space. The boredom may also fluctuate between mild and intense. What is happening is a form of catharsis that is long overdue. As with any personal emotional work, we should only allow ourselves to experience boredom at a level we feel safe with. We just have to ride the wave, but be prepared for intense feelings.

While it is best to be alone and silent during boredom, our environment may not always cooperate. As long as what is going on around us is not too engaging or distracting, boredom will still come. There is no right way to sit, or to be while you are trying to be bored. You should be comfortable and try not to move around too much. I prefer having my eyes open and staring out the window. In general, I do not close my eyes, but this may work for some of you.

BUILDING YOUR BOREDOM TOLERANCE

As a consequence of living in an age of so many distractions, we need to consciously build up our tolerance for boredom before we can use it to create an amazing life. When we have alcohol on a regular basis, our tolerance for it goes higher and, over time, we need more and more of it to get the same physical and psychological effects. The same is true of coffee. The first cup of coffee we ever have makes us feel a jittery buzz, but after a few of weeks of regular coffee drinking, we can have three sludgy cups and feel almost nothing.

Distraction has the same "building up" effect. The more we distract ourselves from boredom and living an authentic life, the more distractions we need to keep us from facing whatever is in the space of boredom. Most of us have such a high tolerance for distraction and excitement that we need a high level of it to sustain us. However, all this distraction has, conversely, caused a dangerously low tolerance for boredom. The relationship between boredom and distraction is a direct and inverse one. So in order to increase our tolerance for boredom, we need to decrease our distractions. Purposefully increasing spaces of boredom in our lives is the only way to build up our tolerance.

HOW MUCH BOREDOM IS ENOUGH?

When we begin allowing boredom into our lives, we feel discomfort. The amount of discomfort one can tolerate is very individual and depends on how much we have been resisting moments of boredom over the years. To begin to allow boredom into our lives, we can start with shorter moments of boredom and see where it takes us. As I mentioned before, boredom causes physiological stress, so we need to be gentle with ourselves when we experience the discomfort. There is no right or wrong way to handle your boredom. If you have a trusted friend, partner, or counsellor, maybe make time to reflect on the feelings that came up for you during the spaces of boredom afterwards. The more tolerant you become of boredom, the more it will reveal to you, and the longer you can be with it. I highly recommend having emotional support available from someone who knows that you are trying to shift your relationship with boredom.

TUNING IN TO BOREDOM

Once we are able to allow longer spaces of boredom into our lives, we will begin to notice different thoughts and feelings emerge from that space. Our boredom has different things to say about our lives, relationships, and personal beliefs.

Heidegger states that the moods we experience are not locked within our bodies, but affect our perceptions of the world around us. These moods *attune* us to certain characteristics of the world. When we are angry, we will almost always find irritation in every person and object. When we are frightened in the middle of the night, almost every noise or unfamiliar object is dangerous. Similarly, when we are bored, some of the things in our lives will reveal their inner meaninglessness to us. If we think of Heidegger's concept of attunement as wearing coloured glasses that give us different views of the world, the experience of boredom is like removing those glasses we have had on all our lives. So when we tune in to boredom, we are tuning in to the purest way of viewing different parts of our lives. By "pureness" I mean what things really mean to us, before our family, culture, or society attached meaning to them. For example, we might place a lot of importance on our social status because of what we have learned from the world over the years. Tuning in to boredom may reveal to us that, although we have spent years working towards increasing our social status, deep down we really don't care.

Lars Svendsen provides a beautiful metaphor that describes how boredom exposes the arbitrary meaning system that we are situated in. He says that before we learn to embrace boredom, we see the world like a whole painting. But after we have moved into the deep spaces of boredom, the whole of the picture is gone. What we now see is the individual blots of paint that don't give us meaning themselves, but only as part of the painting. However, if we view the painting as our lives, we now have the power to take all those blots of paint and move them around to create our own meaning. This is the power of boredom. The more bored we get, the clearer it becomes to us which personal meanings in our lives need to be reevaluated. Within the spaces of boredom, we might find problematic worldviews and negative personal beliefs. In this way, boredom attunes us to the deeper, more unconscious levels of ourselves. Therefore, it's important not to judge the feelings and thoughts that come to us because we might try to resist them. Instead, let boredom do its work.

THE MESSAGES WITHIN BOREDOM

There are different types of messages that we are likely to become aware of in the spaces of boredom. First, you may sense or feel the complete arbitrariness of different things in your life. This might lead to the realization that wearing a different outfit every day is completely pointless to you. And you would be right. I mean, if an alien came to earth, would it change its outfit every day? Is it some universal rule that we must change our outfit every day? It is only important because we place this act in the context of our meaning system.

During our times of boredom, we may also become more aware of negative beliefs about ourselves. These are the beliefs that we have never really explored, yet deeply accepted. While we can never completely detach ourselves from these beliefs, it is imperative that we explore these beliefs and become aware of how they are affecting us.

DECONSTRUCTING THE MESSAGES

The meanings that we become aware of in the space of boredom can be *deconstructed*. This term was coined by French philosopher Jacques Derrida. It is the process of finding the underlying assumptions in any given text or message. In our case, we want to understand the underlying assumptions of the negative messages we are experiencing in the space of boredom. For example, during times of boredom, some of us may feel the intense desire to call someone. In this scenario, the emotion that may have surfaced within the space of boredom (and that we may not be consciously aware of) could be loneliness. We can only become aware of this if we remain in the space of boredom, instead of distracting ourselves from it by picking up our phones. By staying with our boredom for longer, we can deconstruct and discover what meanings or beliefs we are unconsciously accepting. Here are a few example questions that we could ask ourselves to help deconstruct the meanings:

What do I believe will get rid of my negative feeling?

> ► Talking to someone would cure my loneliness

What is a belief I have about myself that may have triggered this feeling?

> ► I am not outgoing/likeable/good enough

What societal ideals may have created this belief?

> ► It is important to be liked by many people
> ► Having many friends and being social means you are likeable
> ► Having many people around leads to happiness
> ► Having an outgoing or extroverted personality is more likable

Think of exceptions or examples that debunk the ideas above.

> ► No one can be liked by everyone

- ▶ Being social with many people is not necessarily equal to having meaningful connections
- ▶ There are many popular people who are unhappy
- ▶ There are many kind, valuable, intelligent introverted people in the world

GOING DOWN THE RABBIT HOLE

Attuning yourself to meanings through boredom is a cumulative and compounding journey. The insights and realizations that you have about yourself and your personal beliefs reveal even deeper insights the next time. The horizons of boredom are ever expanding and plunge us deeper into existence.

Now, we may ask ourselves why we would want to realize that a lot of our perceptions and beliefs lack any purpose in life. This is because it's not that we don't have any meaning or purpose, but that we have the power to shift it and change it as we please. That is what life is all about, moving from meaning to meaning as we change and grow. What was important to you ten years ago, may not be important to you now. Boredom helps you to realize the freedom you have to give meaning to all things in your life, including yourself. It unlocks us from the chains of the meaning systems that we were born into.

"And there is a time, glorious too in its own way, when one scarcely exists, when one is a complete void. I mean—when boredom seems the very stuff of life."
— *Henry Miller*

Chapter 6

THE IMPORTANCE OF BOREDOM IN DAILY LIFE

We all want to live meaningful and fulfilling lives, but because of all the diversions, distractions, and our unwillingness to be bored, we never get the chance to truly explore what that means for us. Boredom provides us with the space and time to make our lives a work of art. Boredom is a multifaceted space that can help us to create the life we truly want. In this chapter, we'll explore the different ways that boredom will help you to finally achieve the goals that are important to you and create a life that is uniquely meaningful and satisfying to you.

BOREDOM DESTROYS OUR LIMITATIONS

To have a fulfilling life, we must live within a system of meaning. However, before we can create a meaning system that works for us, we must destroy the one that underlies a dissatisfying life. For example, if our dissatisfaction in life arose because of specific, unexamined ideas of what we believe "success" is, we need to redefine success for ourselves before we can move forward with creating a more meaningful life. Embracing boredom helps us to destroy the limiting, restrictive worldviews and personal beliefs that prevent us from living our best life.

BOREDOM IS THE INFINITE SPACE FOR CREATING OUR LIVES

Some of us believe there is an ultimate, universal, or "perfect" state of happiness, fulfillment, and bliss. We believe that if we could only find the right spiritual path, or make x amount of money that we would be able to experience this perpetual state of happiness. First of all, this does not make conceptual sense because without experiencing pain and suffering, we cannot know what happiness feels like. It would just be "it" because we have nothing to compare it to. Boredom prevents us from falling into this trap. Boredom reminds us that there will always be a gap between the ideal utopian state in our minds and the reality of our lives. Boredom helps us realize that, at different times, everything can be boring (or meaningless) to us. There is nothing that will keep us continuously and happily engaged. When we realize this, our happiness no longer depends on finding the one perfect thing that will stop us from ever being bored again. Instead, we realize that we are free to fill the space of boredom with whatever we want and, in turn, create what we want with this infinite space that is suddenly available to us.

WE CREATE OUR PERSONAL STORY USING BOREDOM

When we are bored, things in our lives no longer seem to fit together. It is like we are viewing our lives from the outside. In life, many of us are living a story that we accepted from our families, cultures, and societies, with the belief that living this way would provide us with perpetual meaning and satisfaction. Boredom helps us realize that these stories are only stories. The stories don't make sense when we are bored, and we don't understand why meaning has disappeared. We get confused because we followed all the rules, yet boredom is still there sometimes. This is one of the reasons why we don't like to be bored. It is the ultimate reminder that all these things don't provide continuous bliss. But what boredom is whispering to you is, "Hey! Don't you get it? You need to write your own story. You are the only one who knows what the happy ending is."

In the movie *Stranger Than Fiction*, Harold Crick's (Will Ferrell) life is governed by a narrator that only he and the moviegoer can hear. She governs his every move. She is like the voice in our subconscious telling us how to live our lives. Eventually, Harold realizes that the narrator is leading him to live an inauthentic life that is not his own and so he tries to change the story before it is too late. Boredom allows us to see the story that has been written for our lives thus far, but also shows us that, with this awareness, we can begin to create a new story.

Rollo May says the world is a pattern of meaningful relations in which we exist and participate. Boredom allows space in your day for your mind to wander and your imagination to expand without it being wrenched back into the reality of the world by some distraction. If you let it, the space of boredom will help you to create meaningful visions for your life. The more you let the spaces of boredom into your life, the more personal insights will enter into that space.

FILLING UP THE SPACE OF BOREDOM

Once we let boredom break down our limiting worldviews, we can begin to create or fill up our lives again. But this time, we do it on own terms. Before, our spaces of boredom were filled up with thoughts, ideas, and activities that were somewhat unexamined. Now that we are aware of this, we have the power to fill up our boredom intentionally, so we can live with meaning and fulfillment.

While there are no rules about what you should fill your life with, the awareness of your reactions to boredom should guide you. Let me be clear. There is absolutely nothing wrong with having a few drinks, travelling to a tropical place, or binge watching a show on Netflix. This book isn't about defining what is right or wrong. It isn't about telling you what the "right" thing to fill the space of boredom with is. But what is important is that you are aware of your own personal reasons for doing those things and that you consciously choose to fill your boredom with the best activity for you at that moment. Once we have reflected on what we want our lives to look like, we can use the spaces of boredom to evaluate and revise our vision whenever we feel we need to.

BOREDOM INCREASES PLEASURE

When creating our lives, there are three modes of being to be aware of. Most of our day is made up of two modes of being: the *creative mode* and the *consumptive mode*. Some examples of the creative mode are times when we are at work, studying, cleaning, or performing other necessary chores. Activities that are consumptive are things such as eating, watching TV, having a glass of wine, and reading. Both the creative and consumptive modes are animalistic drives that have kept us alive for millennia. However, these two modes of being distract us from a very important third mode—boredom.

It is important that we have moments of boredom in our lives because it is what tempers the other two modes, and stops them from taking over our lives. It has become all too easy these days to let activities take over our lives. Boredom isn't just a valuable tool, it is also a mode of human existence that should be included in daily life just like creation or consumption.

Boredom is what makes the other two modes more pleasurable and exciting. The more we consume food, drink, people, products, or places to feel meaning and pleasure, the sooner they lose their luster. When we are constantly creating, working, and foraging for something new, we will get burnt out. Boredom allows us the space and time for us to pause, reflect, and see the big picture of life again. In a way, we need to have a break from both creation and consumption so they can provide us pleasure again. This is why going from pleasurable activity to pleasurable activity will eventually lead to less satisfaction.

BOREDOM INCREASES MEANING

In the same way boredom increases our pleasure when doing daily activities, it also increases meaning in our lives. It does this by providing us a break from things that are meaningful so we can appreciate them again. After an hour of sitting and doing nothing, even a simple walk to the store can fill you with joy. The leaves on the trees will seem more vivid and green, and you may even begin to notice the caress of the breeze on your skin. Over time, the more you let boredom into your life, the more the world around you will come alive.

When I get tired of things I am normally passionate about, I allow myself to just be in the space of boredom and, after a while, the feelings of passion are renewed and I am ready to engage in them again. I would advise allowing spaces of boredom in your day after intense moments of engagement to ground yourself and to prevent yourself from swinging intensely from the creative mode to the consumptive mode, and back again. It will provide you with more fulfillment in all areas of your life. It will even make previously "boring activities" more engaging.

BOREDOM INCREASES PHILOSOPHICAL AWARENESS

Boredom has been called the most philosophical of moods. It allows us to grapple with Heidegger's perennial question: Why is there something rather than nothing? According to Socrates, and many others, an important element required for life satisfaction and meaning is the contemplation of existence. Boredom brings the paradoxes of our lives to the fore and forces us deeper into life.

Every time we allow ourselves to be bored, we allow the opportunity to gain insight into life, the world, and existence. As we allow more and more boredom into our lives, these insights begin to interact and compound to reveal new and deeper insights. Boredom is a never ending spiral of personal and philosophical discoveries that can be used to create a great life.

BOREDOM IS A SPIRITUAL PRACTICE

Boredom is the space and time when the sheer awesomeness and mystery of the universe is revealed to us. It uncovers the essential truth that we are beings who are hurling through an unknown universe. It is important to contemplate the cosmic level of our existence because it helps us to put events in our lives in perspective and, thus, helps to relieve the stresses of daily life.

In his book, *Janus: A Summing Up*, Arthur Koestler describes his moments alone while in solitary confinement, not knowing if he was going to die at any moment. He says that these moments "filled [him] with a direct certainty that a higher order of reality existed and that it alone invested existence with meaning." While grappling with his mortality, and having nothing to distract him during his long periods of solitude, Koestler gained spiritual insights that seemed to come from somewhere outside himself.

Boredom also dissolves the boundaries of our egos. The deeper we go into boredom, the more we feel our identities becoming fluid and contingent. We begin to realize that our identity only means something within the constructed meaning system, and when that falls away, so does the self.

These days, many of us feel a desire to connect to nature. Boredom returns us to the speed and rhythm of nature. We'll take walks in the forest, meditate outside, or even build a cabin in the middle of nowhere. One might argue that the therapeutic benefits of being in nature, aside from the good air and soothing sounds, arises because we return to the speed of nature in our minds. Thus, we don't necessarily need to go anywhere to receive these benefits. We can slow ourselves to the rhythm of nature just by being in the space of boredom. Trees grow for thousands of years, clouds move across the sky at a slow pace, and rivers, while swift at times, migrate over millennia. Boredom slows life down so much that time almost stops. It is within the space of boredom that we can feel most in touch with the rhythm of the natural world around us.

"It is possible for boredom to deliver us to our best selves, the ones that long for risk and illumination and unspeakable beauty. If we sit still long enough, we may hear the call behind boredom. With practice, we may have the imagination to rise up from the emptiness and answer." — Nancy H. Blakey

"The Gods were bored; therefore, they created human beings."
— Soren Kierkegaard

Chapter 7
THE POWERFUL RELATIONSHIP BETWEEN BOREDOM AND CREATIVITY

WHY CREATIVITY IS IMPORTANT

In his great work, *The Courage to Create*, American psychologist Rollo May relates creativity and the creative process to the human fight or flight response. When our bodies respond to something with fight or flight, it is usually because we encounter something that threatens us. We become completely focused and engaged in what we are doing because we need to in order to survive. An important outcome of this is an extreme focus and engagement, which also gives us a deep sense of meaning. This is because when we are struggling for survival, we are always engaged with the purpose of surviving and, therefore, always have meaning. Rollo May asserts that the creative process is very similar to the fight or flight response because it keeps us focused and engaged and therefore, provides us with deep and profound meaning.

CREATIVITY IS YOUR OWN PERSONAL WAR

Creativity is an attempt to bring something new into the world. It is not merely painting by numbers or making something. Rollo May describes creativity as "the encounter with the intensively conscious human being with his or her world." In other words, creativity is really about us fulfilling our existence in the world by sharing our unique selves. However, like I mentioned above, the creative act is also a lot like the experience of survival. It is a deep impulse like the desire to eat or have sex and so, on some level, it is part of our nature. Today, it is one of the only ways we can mimic our deep instinct for survival. By creating, we are not fighting animals or harsh climates. We are warding off an even fiercer opponent. Meaninglessness.

When we are engaged in the creative process, we deal with others who don't understand our vision. We encounter discouragement, negative opinions, and even those who will call us crazy. They may get angry, resentful, and even hateful. Some will tell us to stop wasting our time and get back to "real" life. It becomes a constant internal battle as we attempt to keep ourselves faithful to our vision.

We are also at war with ourselves. We are in an epic and ongoing battle with our idea of perfection. Our vision will never be fully realized. No painting ever fulfills the painter's expectations. No author is ever totally satisfied with their story. No mathematician ever stops searching for a more elegant solution to a problem. We never fully achieve what we set out to do, but we keep waging the war anyway. The vision is so compelling to us that we want to see how close we can get to perfection. This is an ongoing battle that keeps us engaged for a lifetime. When we feel we are losing the battle, self-doubt and the pull to give up our vision are potent poisons that haunt us. They are part of the territory. These inevitable aspects of the creative process mimic the struggle for survival, as if we are at war on several fronts.

YOU CANNOT CREATE WITHOUT BOREDOM

To live a meaningful life, we need to express ourselves creatively. However, there is one thing standing in our way: our unwillingness to be bored and our penchant for constant distraction. In fact, creativity withers and dies with constant busyness, but boredom is the mother of the creative act.

There are many proponents of the view that boredom is necessary, if not imperative for the creative development of both children and adults. Dr. Teresa Belton and Dr. Esther Priyadharshini describe boredom as a "stimulus to new thinking and action." The role boredom has on creativity has been increasingly discussed because of the recent shift from children having unscheduled play time, to having prescribed activities filling up their days. In an article in Newsweek magazine, Anna Quindlen advocates for allowing children to have more of the unstructured play time because of the way it stimulates imagination. There is no doubt that there is a powerful relationship between boredom and creativity. The ability to embrace boredom is essential for true creativity to emerge.

CREATIVE IDEAS EMERGE FROM BOREDOM

The funny thing about creative ideas is that they hardly ever present themselves when we want them too. When we are intensely concentrating on finding a creative solution to a problem, the answer doesn't come while we are thinking about it. Instead, the answer comes when our minds are not engaged in anything. This is because creativity is largely an unconscious process. When we think hard about a problem, we only see a limited view of it. However, while we are bored, our unconscious mind is working with the vast amount of information and experience from our entire lives. Some theorists even believe that creativity does not actually come from within, but comes from someplace beyond. However, many agree that most great ideas and creative breakthroughs come "out of the blue" when our minds are not focused. Great ideas come when we are most able to let our unconscious thought processes come to the surface. These are during moments of boredom. By being bored, we allow the space for new ideas and breakthroughs to come. Our creative ideas cannot emerge if we fill the space of boredom with activity and distractions. In a conversation, if you are always talking, the other person will never get a chance to speak. As soon as you are quiet for a few minutes, they fill the silence with their ideas. Given the chance, your unconscious will provide creative ideas for you in the space of boredom.

BOREDOM IS A CREATIVE SPACE

When we experience boredom, we are faced with an empty space. We can imagine this space as a blank canvas. A blank canvas on which to begin creating.

Boredom also provides a space where ideas can grow and develop. Within boredom, all of the information within you has a chance to incubate and mix with all the other information in your unconscious. This is when the magic happens. Similar to the process of baking, we must mix the ingredients (or thoughts) together before our dish (or insight) is ready. With heat, there is a chemical reaction that transforms the ingredients into something completely new.

Another reason why boredom is a potent space for creation is because it switches our minds to superhuman escape mode. Our minds do not like boredom, and so they will do almost anything to escape it. It will muster up all its power and creativity to get itself engaged in something again. This is similar to when people seem to suddenly gain an unusually high level of strength or courage when faced with dangerous or desperate situations. When we resist external engagement, then our minds come up with increasingly creative ways to get us engaged. This is where great ideas and breakthroughs come from.

Another way to look at this is to think back to Lars Svendsen's painting metaphor that I mentioned before. When we are bored, we see all our thoughts as blots of paint, not a part of the painting itself. Each blot lacks meaning beyond its own existence. When we are able to reach the deep level of boredom that gets us to this place, we can then put the pieces back together in any way we like. Picasso has said that "every act of creation is first of all an act of destruction." In order to create something new, we must destroy the old ways of understanding it. We must shed it of its old meanings. If we want to create something new, we can't stick with the old ways of looking at things. The ultimate destruction is the breakdown of all the systems of meaning that happens within boredom.

Boredom helps us to become an intensively conscious person so we can engage in extraordinary creative acts. This is because the space of boredom removes all of our previous meanings and allows us to break new ground through creativity. Boredom is the ultimate creative space for the mind.

TUNING IN TO BOREDOM FOR CREATIVE INSIGHTS

As part of the creative war we are fighting, there are negative thoughts and feelings that will invade our space of boredom, clogging it up so that it is far less likely that our ideas will emerge. Thus, these negative thoughts and feelings must be dealt with before we can use boredom effectively for creative insights. This is an ongoing process and can't be completely resolved before beginning the creative process. Instead, the awareness of these negative thoughts and feelings helps us to identify them as such so we can push them aside and receive creative insights.

We can't tell boredom what to do, but we can gently coax it like a dream. Here's what I mean. When we watch horror movies before bed, it is far more likely that our dreams will take on the theme of horror. After we have had a particularly stressful week, our dreams are likely to reflect that as well. Likewise, we can "front load" our boredom by filling our minds with specific information for our unconscious to digest during moments of boredom. During the process of writing this book, I have made the conscious habit of immersing myself throughout the day in books and articles about boredom. I'm finding that when I get bored, it all comes back to me in new and exciting formations that I voraciously write down. It's quite exhilarating to say the least.

IF YOU GET BORED, YOU ARE CREATIVE

Creativity is a built-in impulse that all of us have. So why do some people seem more creative than others? For a few reasons. First, modern society with all its distractions, coupled with the glorification of busyness have dulled our ability to allow our unique creativity to emerge. In today's society, we must choose to be creative, just as we must choose to be bored. All people are creative by nature and no one is more creative than anyone else. Being creative does not necessarily limit us to specific vocations such as painter, writer, scientist, or architect. Remember that the truly creative act is bringing something new into the world that pushes the boundaries of what came before. It is a unique solution to a problem, or seeing something in a completely new way. It could be coming up with a new recipe that has half of the calories but all the flavour. Creative acts can be achieved in almost any job. Finding creative solutions to problems or finding new approaches to standard systems are all amazing, innovative forms of creativity. In the end, all you really need is yourself because the art of self-creation is the most creative act.

"Boredom is therefore a vital problem for the moralist since at least half of the sins of mankind are caused by the fear of it."
— *Bertrand Russell*

"A generation that cannot endure boredom will be a generation of little men."
— *Bertrand Russell*

Chapter 8

BOREDOM: AN ETHICAL PRACTICE

At first, it may seem strange to contemplate the exploratory and experiential aspects of boredom through an ethical lens. However, when we actually think about it, boredom has been a significant influence on both great creative and innovative accomplishments, as well as the most horrendous acts of evil and destruction. A quick search of quotes about boredom on the internet reveals this contrast. Kierkegaard advocates for avoiding boredom because it is the root of all evil, while Nietzsche claims that avoiding boredom will mess up our lives. Until recently, boredom has received very little attention and so it has never really been considered as a ground for ethical decisions in our lives. However, with our diminishing tolerance for boredom, it is crucial for us to explore the ethical implications of boredom (or the lack of it) in our lives.

TO BE ETHICAL, WE MUST BE AWARE OF OUR BOREDOM

When we live lives driven by wanderlust, restlessness, hedonism, or a dangerous devotion to a cause, we are often avoiding the space of boredom. There is a fear of facing the meaninglessness revealed in that space. So if we are driven by this fear, who is actually calling the shots? Is it you, or is it the fear of boredom that is pulling at your strings? Can we be ethical people if there is something else, like fear, running our lives?

If this need to escape boredom is one of the root causes of our behaviors then, to be ethical, we must fulfill our moral obligation to learn how we react to it. Here is why. Michel Foucault, the French philosopher, explains that freedom is a necessary precondition for ethical behaviour. However, we can't free ourselves from forces affecting our behaviours if we aren't aware them. Therefore, we must first gain awareness of what is stopping us from acting ethically so we can then be free to do so. So it is our moral imperative to become aware of our destructive reactions to boredom so we can do something about them, and free ourselves to act ethically.

BOREDOM PREVENTS OBJECTIFICATION OF OTHERS AND ALLOWS US TO BE KIND

Objectification is a concept that the modern world abhors. Articles all over the internet condemn the objectification of women in advertisements, and the objectification of child laborers in third world countries. When we objectify others, we are essentially viewing them as objects or "things". None of us want to believe that we are capable of objectifying others. We don't want to believe that we are capable of treating others as objects. Surely we know the difference between a valued human and, say, a pencil! Objectification of humans disturbs us because we see how it leads to all kinds of inhumane ways of treating people. So what causes objectification?

Essentially, when people are objectified, they become a means to an end, rather than a valuable individual in and of themselves. Often subconsciously, we justify our view of them because we need them to serve a need of ours. When we do this, we are unable to empathize with them and treat them with the respect and care that we want to. Objectification can be viewed as the opposite of empathy because we are incapable of empathizing with someone who we have already categorized as a means to an end. Interestingly, our relationship with boredom has a huge influence on how much we objectify others in our lives.

One extreme way we avoid boredom is by filling our time with people. As I mentioned before, one of the ways we might deal with negative emotions that surface in the space of boredom is by impulsively calling or texting others so we don't have to face those emotions. Other times we may suddenly feel the urge to make plans with family or friends to fill our time. I'm all for spending quality time with family and friends, but that isn't what I'm talking about. Under the guise of "quality time with loved ones", these situations are created to avoid the thoughts and emotions that might surface in the space of boredom.

How do you know? When you want the party to go on until you're too tired or drunk to be conscious of the discomfort of boredom. Maybe you want it to go on forever because the thought of trying to find another stimulating activity to keep you engaged is extremely painful.

When we use people to avoid the spaces of boredom, they become objects to us. They almost become our possessions. They become a means to an end. What we are really thinking when we are with them is: "Love me!" or "Entertain me!" or "Save me!" When we are avoiding boredom, we don't view others as valuable beings with needs of their own. In fact, during these times, we really couldn't less about their happiness or personal needs as long as they fulfill their roles as pleasant distractions for us. They become another "thing" to distract us from the space of boredom. Of course we don't objectify people all the time, and there are times when we do need people to help us or to give us emotional support. This isn't what I'm talking about here. I'm talking about unconsciously using people to fill our time without much care for the enjoyment or consequences to them, because we are desperately avoiding boredom.

In this scenario, we don't want to see our loved ones because we enjoy sharing our mutual love or because we want to learn their thoughts and dreams, but because we are avoiding boredom like the plague. Our need to avoid boredom is so strong that we are unintentionally objectifying important people in our lives and, as a consequence, we are unable to love or care for them in the authentic way we want to. How can we when they are only there to distract us from boredom? We have reduced our loved ones to the same level as a TV show, social media, or anything else that will keep us engaged as we avoid boredom. Thus, if we want to treat others humanely, we must make it a priority to be aware of our potentially toxic reactions to boredom.

BOREDOM CONNECTS PEOPLE

Rene Descartes and Baruch Spinoza, both enlightenment philosophers, believed that we behave unethically because of insufficient knowledge of life and existence. Similarly, Socrates believed that no one actually wants to be unethical, but that we could act more ethically if we gained more knowledge of the "truth". In other words, to act ethically, we need to be willing to think and learn about a situation as much as possible before taking action. As I have discussed before, the most important truths about existence are revealed in the spaces of boredom and these truths help us to make better decisions in life.

The scariest, yet most profound knowledge that boredom provides us is the fact that all the meanings we attach to events, objects, and people are completely arbitrary. However, even though we know the contingent nature of our meaning systems, we still need meaning to live. We are meaning seeking creatures in a universe where no ultimate meaning is apparent. This knowledge, that there is no ultimate meaning, is the most important ethical ground in the modern world. I will explain why.

Our meaning systems protect us from the scary nothingness of existence. They are our comfort because they provide a sense of certainty in an unexplainable universe. The meaning systems that we are born into reach deep into our minds, bodies, and souls. They are so entrenched at almost every level of our lives that it is impossible to ever completely separate ourselves from them.

For a moment, consider the alternative, that we don't believe our personal meaning system is arbitrary. That we believe that our beliefs are universal truths. What happens when we meet someone who threatens our meaning system by questioning its validity? We will be met with a deep internal conflict as our sense of certainty is shaken. We will do almost anything to make our meaning system stable again. We will argue, fight, and maybe try to convince ourselves that we are right and the other person is wrong, even though deep inside we don't really know. How many wars have been fought over belief systems because one side believes they are in possession of the truth? We are so dependent on our meaning system for comfort that we will do almost anything to ensure they are right, even killing those who don't agree. But eliminating those who threaten it does not make our meaning system right. It just means we don't have to face the possibility that it is wrong. We categorize others who believe a different truth as unaware, lesser than, infidels, or testers of faith. In fact, a common reaction to an outside threat is to have even more conviction about our own meaning system as we fight, not for our views, but for our sense of certainty.

Political beliefs are much the same way. They are a meaning-system just like a religion, but also arbitrary. They help us make our way in an uncertain world. Do we despise the other side because of their beliefs, or because they are a threat to our view of the world?

The other side must be inherently wrong because if they are not, then our entire way of being is under threat. So we treat them as evil, ignorant, and even dangerous. Thus, when we view our personal beliefs and meanings as truth, we leave our sense of self vulnerable for times when those beliefs are threatened. Also, rather than viewing others as humans with the same existential plight as ourselves, we create divides between each other as we ferociously defend our personal truths.

On the other hand, becoming comfortable with the space of boredom helps us to experience the arbitrary nature of our meaning systems and provides an important ethical ground. The space of boredom brings the realization that our meanings are no better than any other. That all meaning systems are equal in the space of boredom. This knowledge reduces the dogmatism that leads to a lot of the violence and atrocities of our world, and allows us to connect with others through understanding and compassion.

When we realize that all of us are in the same predicament of having to create meaning systems for ourselves and that some of us are thrown into meaning systems where we don't fit so well, we cannot help but to have empathy. Sure, the behaviours and actions of some may not be acceptable to you, but you have a good understanding of the reasons behind their actions. They are the same as yours.

"In an age of speed, I began to think nothing could be more exhilarating than going slow. In an age of distraction, nothing can feel more luxurious than paying attention. And in an age of constant movement, nothing is more urgent than sitting still."

— *Pico Iyer*

Chapter 9
FINAL THOUGHTS

BOREDOM: A SPACE VOID OF MEANING

The Bare Naked Ladies lyrics "alone and bored on a 30th century night" from the song *It's all been done before*, perfectly sums up how many of us feel in the modern world—bored. In fact, the more advancement and progress we have as a species, the more boring our lives seem to become. But why is this? Shouldn't a future with unbridled technology be exciting and meaningful?

On the surface, the relationship between boredom and meaning seems simple. Meaning is finding something that is worthwhile to do with our time, something that we believe will lead to satisfaction or security. So when we're bored, it's a sign that we are not finding anything meaningful at the moment. Lars Svendsen says "emptiness of time is an emptiness of meaning." Boredom feels like an emptiness, or a longing. The emptiness is quite possibly a result of instincts carried over from our hunter-gatherer days telling our bodies and brains we should be doing something purposeful that will ensure our survival. A *movement-toward-survival* is probably a genetic imperative, but the problem today is that for many of us in the post-industrial world, our daily activities are no longer centered on physical survival.

SURVIVAL AND THE BIRTH OF EXISTENTIAL BOREDOM

In our modern world, our survival is pretty much guaranteed. But this isn't necessarily a good thing. In fact, this is why both Svendsen and Frankl agree that beyond survival, we begin to experience boredom, and it is at this point when we must find a reason for being. This is also why when we reach a goal the thrill of achievement fades quickly. Once we have guaranteed our survival, our existence becomes a bit of a problem to figure out. We busy ourselves chasing experiences, food, people, and money, and tell ourselves they are necessary and important. However, in excess, eventually their returns diminish. Our bodies and minds scream out "*now what*?!".

Day in and day out, our hunter-gatherer ancestors worked on activities required for survival. There was no point in getting bogged down with asking why we exist. Hence, while they may have experienced situational boredom, they likely experienced very little (if any) existential boredom. Thus, one of the main problems for us today is that we are just so far removed from our baseline survival needs that our lives have just become time filling, busyness, and distraction.

BOREDOM DURING THE COVID-19 PANDEMIC

The COVID-19 pandemic highlighted just how intolerable boredom has become for us and how powerful it is as an emotional state and experience. This was probably the first time in modern history, that we were forced to confront long periods of empty spaces in time. How did you handle it?

Suddenly our lives lost the bulk of the content that filled our days. Some experienced this as loss and grief as we mourned the loss of our distractions, time fillers, and pleasures. In essence, it was a loss of our identities. Others spoke of the trauma of feeling uncertainty and a loss of security. Every surface, enclosed space, and person became a threat of death and disease.

The self-avoidance that was veiled by frivolous activities was ripped away and things became serious. Our sense of trust in our world and way of life was gone; something that most us have never experienced. We also realized that the whole structure of our society was far more fragile than we ever imagined. It was the end of the illusion that our society was an enduring entity. Most of all, the boredom exposed the fact that many of us rely on meaningless distractions to cope with our mental and emotional struggles more than we'd like to admit. We were forced to quit these distractions cold turkey, and the discomfort brought our addictions to the surface as we, like any addicts, desperately filled our time up with whatever we could find. Some become workaholics, others baked copious amounts of sourdough bread. Many used the opportunity to get in shape.

If we allowed the boredom to linger a bit longer, the space brought into awareness how little meaning many of our pre-COVID activities were providing us, and so purposeful action was taken; quitting jobs, rediscovering creative pursuits, and just living with more intention. The COVID-19 pandemic showed us how much we avoid boredom, and if consciously paid attention to, how powerful it can be in transforming our lives.

HONOURING BOREDOM

It is so easy to be distracted from life in our world today. We think that all the busyness and diversion is all that life has to offer. Many of us figure that if we fill up our day with a much as possible, we will live meaningful and satisfying lives. But we never stop to think of what we are filling our lives with and why. We simply accept the default life. The "McMeanings." It is no wonder that so many of us feel so unfulfilled.

If we are brave enough to let it into our lives, boredom offers a way out of this predicament. It is a powerful mood that is capable of driving us to great feats of creativity or terrible acts of destruction. This is why it is the most powerful human emotion. The awareness of our reactions to it has a direct influence on the quality of our lives and the lives of others. We can use it as the powerful form of meditation that it is. It can free us of limiting personal beliefs and worldviews that stop us from living well. Most profoundly, the space of boredom reveals to us that the meaning we attach to ourselves, events, and our world are conditional and arbitrary. It reveals that nothing has any meaning beyond its own existence. But rather than being something negative, this is the most liber-ating and exciting realization that a person can have. It means that you are free to create yourself.

Just like an artist is never able to realize their ideal vision, we cannot expect to ever find perfect bliss, our ideal self, or a perfect meaning that does not fade. However, it is this limitation that gives life its zest. It is the quest for the perfect existence that keeps life interesting. Imagine how bored we would be if we achieved perfect bliss, enlightenment, and immortality. For humans, it is always about the struggle for something. The carrot that we can never quite reach. For me, novelty comes with new insights and creative projects that stream from my boredom. It is like trying to find the end of the rainbow. You may never get there but the journey is amazing.

We cannot get rid of absurdity or boredom. The two are always together. Embrace boredom and the absurdity that comes with it. Feel them right down to your bones. This is when you are the most human. Our society has come to a critical point of distraction and diversion because we are so desperate for meaning, but have no idea where to find it. Our tolerance for diversion and engagement has become so high that we seem to need more and more conflict to make our lives feel meaningful. If things don't change, our constant wars on everything may only get worse. We are all subconsciously trying to find meaning and engagement, grabbing onto anything. Ironically, all the distractions are preventing us from finding and creating a truly compelling life.

In the midst of all this dangerous distraction, there are some who are becoming more mindful of being. There are signs that the wall of distraction is beginning to crack. Recently, in South Korea, doing nothing has become a competitive sport. Participants compete to see who can do nothing the longest. The goal is to simply be. It is a collective embrace of boredom. I am optimistic that we are beginning to realize the danger of constant distraction and engagement, and I am hopeful that increasing awareness of boredom will contribute to a more meaningful life and a better world for us all.

So stop distracting yourself from life and start living it.

AFTERWORD

Schopenhauer said this about life: "Life swings like a pendulum backward and forward between pain and boredom."

At first glance, our lives may seem complicated, but what Schopenhauer said captures the essence of our lives. While animal desires are controlled by the reins of instinct, human desires have an infinite nature which pure instinct is unable to control. No matter how much wealth and fame we may have, we become envious of others who have more, and end up feeling dissatisfied with our lives. However, even after some of us obtain more wealth and fame than we could have ever hoped for, the resulting moments of satisfaction never last very long. New desires capture us again as boredom takes over.

On the other hand, animals do not seem to have to deal with the same level of dissatisfaction as long as their basic instinctual needs are satisfied. Look at cows and how they leisurely relax after meals. Cows seem to enjoy their quiet time leisurely, free from dissatisfaction and boredom. In this respect, we can see that it is only humans who suffer from neurotic desires. Not only that, it appears that humans are the only species that get bored.

To us humans, it is not only unfulfilled desires, but also moments of boredom that cause us psychological discomfort. In order to escape boredom, we humans have come up with numerous ways to entertain and pleasure ourselves such as (but not limited to) hunting, gambling, gaming, and sexual pursuits. We even go so far as to start wars to escape boredom. Many Europeans cheered when World War I broke out because, among other reasons, war was a way to overcome the overwhelming feeling of boredom.

Furthermore, while the subject of desire has been an important topic in philosophy in both the east and the west, the closely related phenomenon of boredom has not been examined by many. While philosophers such as Schopenhauer, Kierkegaard, and Nietzsche have explored boredom at times, they have not dealt with it in earnest as an important philosophical topic. It should be noted that Heidegger has offered a detailed analysis of the feeling of boredom in the book *Fundamental Concepts of Metaphysics*, regarding it as an important "philosophical feeling." Similarly, the book you are holding, Mark A. Hawkins's *The Power of Boredom: Why boredom is essential to creating a meaningful life*, presents important and relevant ideas for our times when dealing with the subject.

As shown in the quote by Schopenhauer at the beginning of the afterward, we regard boredom as a source of overwhelming pain. However, Hawkins highlights the benefits of boredom and suggests that we do not use entertainment or work to escape it, but rather immerse ourselves in it. Hawkins's suggestion is a unique idea that is founded in the insights of Nietzsche and Heidegger. Nietzsche has said the following on boredom:

> The solitary speaks. One receives as a reward for much ennui, ill-humour and boredom, such as a solitude without friends, books, duties, or passion must entail, one harvests those quarters of an hour of the deepest immersion in oneself and nature. He who completely entrenches himself against boredom also entrenches himself against himself: he will never get to drink the most potent refreshing draught from the deepest well of his own being.

Courage to be boring. —Whoever lacks the courage to allow himself and his work to be found boring is certainly not a spirit of the first rank, whether in the arts or the sciences.

For the thinker and for all inventive spirits, boredom is that disagreeable 'lull' of the soul that precedes a happy voyage and cheerful winds; he has to endure it, must *await* its effect on him—precisely *that* is what lesser natures are totally unable to achieve!

All of you who are in love with hectic work and whatever is fast, new, strange – you find it hard to bear yourselves, your diligence is escape and the will to forget yourself.

Modern restlessness increases towards the west, so that Americans look upon the inhabitants of Europe as altogether peace-loving and enjoying beings, whilst in reality they swarm about like wasps and bees. This restlessness is so great that the higher culture cannot mature its fruits, it is as if the seasons followed each other too quickly. For lack of rest our civilization is turning into a new barbarism. At no period have the active, that is, the restless, been of more importance. One of the necessary corrections, therefore, which must be undertaken in the character of humanity is to strengthen the contemplative element on a large scale.

Hawkins and Nietzsche see modern times as an era of anxiety. Such a diagnosis is one that is most fitting for the world today. Today, adults and youth alike are in a constant state of work and study for fear they will fall behind.

Nowadays, we get caught up in feelings of agitation and boredom because of the anxiety producing lifestyles we lead, yet we seldom use moments of boredom to reflect on our lives. Instead, we view boredom as a luxury since most of our days are filled with work, studies, entertainment, or stimulating activities that help relieve the accumulated mental stress. Hawkins, once a teacher in Korea for two years, mentions his experiences as a teacher and how he was amazed at the lifestyles of young Korean students who were scheduled nonstop.

Like Nietzsche, Hawkins sees boredom as an opportunity for life reflection and, therefore, a chance to create a life that is intentional. In this way, Hawkins integrated insights from Nietzsche and Heidegger but also expanded upon them. It is clear throughout the book that Hawkins regards Heidegger's ideas on boredom favorably.

In *The Fundamental Concepts of Metaphysics*, Heidegger divides boredom into three categories but focuses particularly on *profound boredom*. When we're lost in profound boredom, life feels meaningless. He calls this experience *inauthentic existence*. Inauthentic existence is the result of embracing the social values that have been instilled in us through our parents and schools since childhood, without ever spending time to critically reflect on them. This default approach to life often leaves us vulnerable to developing an anxious, comparative consciousness that results in focusing on creating status and superiority based on worldly standards. However, at times we are confounded by such a life when it turns out to be meaningless and we begin to feel lost in the experience of profound boredom.

Hawkins states that profound boredom can place us in a space of nothingness or emptiness as taught in Buddhism. According to Hawkins, this space is not empty, but rather a space that is full of creative possibilities. In other words, it has the potential to lead us to live a life of authenticity by helping us to break away from problematic worldly values. Thus, Hawkins encourages us to immerse ourselves into the space of creative possibilities which boredom opens up for us.

Hawkins's book is written with a straight-forward and humorous style that speaks to the various aspects of boredom as well as the benefits of feeling profound boredom. I would recommend this book to anyone who wants to live a more meaningful life. In particular, I think this book has great significance in modern-day Korea, where people have no time to be bored due to various addictions such as work, gaming, and others.

Park Chan-Kuk
Professor of Philosophy
Seoul National University

MARK A. HAWKINS, PH.D., is an author, educator, and a clinical counsellor. His research focuses on interdisciplinary understandings of meaning and purpose as they relate to human wellbeing. He is the author of *The Mismatched Human: Our Fight for a Meaningful Existence.*

Printed in Great Britain
by Amazon

38460155R00078